A55

SPORT CLIMBS

NORTH WALES ROCK CLIMBING

First published in Great Britain 2010 by Pesda Press
Unit 22, Galeri
Doc Victoria
Caernarfon
Gwynedd
LL55 1SQ

maps based on © OpenStreetMap www.openstreetmap.org
(and) contributors, cc-by-sa www.creativecommons.org

ISBN: 978-1-906095-21-5

Printed in Poland, produced by Polska Book.

Tony Shelmerdine finishing
The Quarrywoman (F6b) Expressway Wall,
Penmaen Head. Photo Michael Doyle.

CONTENTS

Ray Wood and Streaky Desroy
on Dead Moggy Syndrome (F6b)
Flowstone Wall, Penmaen Head.
Photo Michael Doyle.

Acknowledgements

Many pcoplo have assisted with this quide with freely given advice, feedback and with establishing new routes and sharing information. I am deeply indebted and this guidc could not have been produced without them. My apologies if I have missed anyone.

In alphabetical order; Ian Andrews, Dave Bathers, Andy Boorman, Mike Burrows (for new routing and much assistance at Penmaen Head and Penmaenbach Quarry), Tommy Chamings, Norman Clacher (perennial activist and my main co-developer at **Penmaen Head**), Glyn Davidson, Chris Doyle, Angela Findlay (for draft document review, general support and great roast dinners utilising organic pork), Colin Goodey, Francis Gowling, Mike Hammill, Pete Harrison, Perry Hawkins, Guy Keating, Martin Kocsis, Alan James, Elfyn Jones – British Mountaineering Council Cymru access officer (for reviewing the crag access notes and providing the main access and conservation notes), Margaret Lally, Dave Lyon, Bonny Masson, Simon Panton, Chris Parkin (N. Wales Bolt Fund), Dave Prendergast, Lee Proctor, Mick Ryan, Tony Shelmerdine (local guru and general historical database for comment and advice throughout and checking the draft document for accuracy), Richard Wheeldon, Pete White, Sarah Woodhouse (for taking the time to minutely check the draft document for grammar). Thanks to Rab Carrington and Steve Long for feedback on **The Gallery**. For **The Gallery**'s recent makeover, feedback, general assistance and photos, thanks are due to; Paul Evans, Mark Hounslea, Dave Kells, Nadim Siddique, Kevin Stephens and particularly Colin Struthers who has been most helpful. Thanks are also due to all those who submitted grade suggestions and other comments (particularly for Penmaen Head) and those members of Clwyd Mountaineering Club who assisted with a clean up at that venue. Many thanks to Franco Ferrero and Peter Wood of Pesda Press who had faith in the project.

Thanks also to the many climbers who have had the vision and energy to establish new routes (very often financed with their own funds) in the area – without them …

Gareth Buckley on Hitachi Arête (F6a) Penmaenbach Quarry. Photo Pete Wood.

Introduction

In recent years there has been an enormous amount of activity, developing sport climbing crags and new climbing areas along the A55 expressway corridor in North Wales between Llanddulas and Penmaenmawr. With the well-received (but now out of print) last definitive guide being published by Rockfax in May 1997, there has been a clear and pressing need for an updated version. This is what you have in your hands.

The region now stands as a viable area in its own right and although very obviously never coming near to challenging Snowdonia, Anglesey and the Ormes, it now complements them rather than being just a second-best wet weather alternative. It's a fun area with lots of good climbing, much of which is new. It will repay full day visits as well as dipping in and bagging a few routes on the way back from Anglesey or Snowdonia. Scoring highly on the accessibility front, together with the convenience of sport climbing and a non-serious character (in the context of climbing) together with the quality of the routes, its popularity should be assured.

The most significant development in the area in recent years was the discovery of the entirely new **Penmaen Head** in October 2006, overlooking the A55 expressway near Old Colwyn. This venue (more like a collection of seven crags in one concise area) yielded a total of 57 sport climbs and one trad climb. It is already becoming popular due to the quality of the climbing with easy access and a flat base. With grades from F5 to F7a but mainly in the F6s, it is an obvious choice for the lower and mid-grade sport climber and it fills a void in that respect. From 2008–2009, focus shifted to **Llanddulas Cave** with much new routing and rebolting. Many routes, which had their hangers removed and hadn't been climbed for years, were resurrected. With the recent establishment of new routes and bolting within the **Upper Cave** out of the rain, **Llanddulas Cave** is now an all-weather venue and offers 41 routes from F5 to F7c+.

Castle Inn is an established handy and very attractive quality venue and now has 18 routes. The obvious clean wall (**Fine View Wall**) to the left of the main crag, long neglected and never appearing in a guidebook, has recently been developed with a mix of quality sport and trad climbs.

Another crag which has deserved a lot more interest but has never appeared in a guidebook (although a topo was published some years ago) is **The Gallery**. This is an unusual crag immediately off the A55 expressway on the seaward side of the Penmaenbach tunnels. Some 24 routes exist on microdiorite, a rock with excellent friction, aptly described as "slate with friction" by one visitor and likened to Carreg Hylldrem by another. It offers quirky climbing characterised by lay-aways and undercuts. Recently, it has been subject to a renaissance and general refurbishment with some new lower-offs and extra bolts being installed by Colin Struthers and friends. The guide is also supplemented by the established venues of the rather daunting **Notice Board Crag** and **Penmaenbach Quarry** – a crag with a few surprisingly good routes in the lower quarry and an impressive upper slab in the upper quarry.

There's a lot to do and a lot that's new. Go for it and enjoy your climbing safely.

Climbers on a popular Railway Tunnel Wall at Penmaen Head on a fine evening. Photo Michael Doyle.

Using the guide

All the information is presented in a consistent way with the first line of a route description containing all the key information. For example:

 Udder Head ★   **⑥ 15m F6a**

5 is the route number on that sector and will correspond to the numbers on the topo. *Udder Head* is the route name. One star is an indication of quality on a system where no stars may be a worthwhile route and three stars is an exceptionally high-quality route. The six in a hexagon informs you that there are six bolts on the route (only given where I have been able to make a precise count). 15m tells you that the route is 15 metres in length (only included where it has been measured accurately). All the routes in the book are under 25m, except for a few on **The Gallery** and **Notice Board Crag** which are up to 30m long (see: Equipment). The number of bolts also gives a rough indication of length. Finally, F6a is the French grade (UK adjectival and technical grades are given for trad routes and A grades for aid routes).

Sport climbing

It is beyond the scope of this guide to provide instruction in sport climbing. See, among others, the excellent instructional book *Sport Climbing +* by Adrian Berry and Steve McClure (Rockfax) for that. However, the two most critical areas are the initial part of the route prior to clipping the first couple of bolts and lowering off, so a couple of tips may be useful.

Before the leader starts off, the belayer should establish himself near to the rock and in a position so that the leader does not have to step over the rope once started. The belayer should allow a lot of slack ready for clipping the first bolt – there is no point keeping the rope snug if it's not clipped in to anything. Once the leader has clipped the first bolt then the belayer should keep slack to a minimum to minimise the chance of an early ground fall by the leader. This should continue until the second bolt is clipped or preferably the third, then the belayer can move away from the rock and allow reasonable slack. When threading the lower-off, make sure you are attached to the rope at all times at your belay loop with a screwgate karabiner. Do not shout "safe"; you aren't.

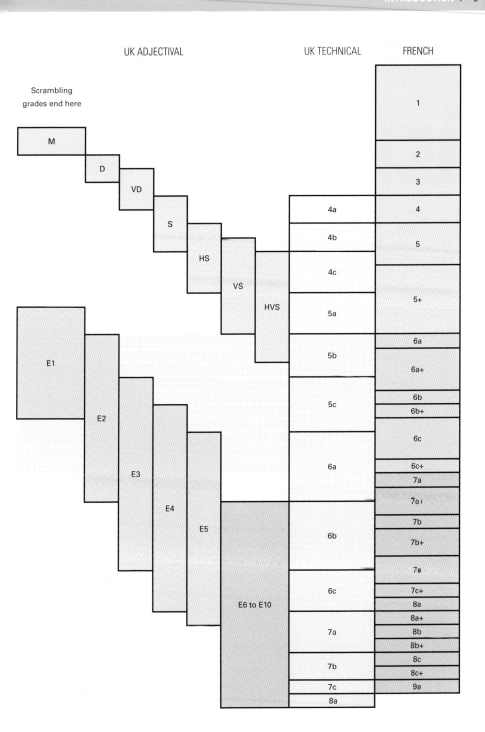

UK ADJECTIVAL   UK TECHNICAL   FRENCH

Scrambling
grades end here

1

M

2

D

3

VD

4a   4

S

4b   5

HS

4c

VS

5+

HVS   5a

6a

5b

6a+

E1

6b

5c

6b+

E2

6c

E3   6a   6c+

7a

E4   7a|

7b

E5   6b

7b+

7e

E6 to E10   6c   7c+

8a

7a   8a+

8b

8b+

8c

7b   8c+

7c   9a

8a

"Safe" is the signal for the belayer to stop belaying and as you are at the top of the route then it could be that is the last thing you want. Thread the lower-off methodically and then check everything. Finally, weight the rope before unclipping from the lower-off. That will confirm that you are actually on the end and that your belayer isn't waiting for you down the pub.

A useful technique to avoid being turned upside down in a fall is to try to keep the rope in front of your leg (avoid allowing the rope to run behind) whilst you climb. This will minimise the chance your leg becoming hooked on the rope. When moving up on lead, let the rope run in the joint between your foot and ankle as much as possible, thereby keeping it at the front.

Grades

All sport climbing grades given are French grades. It does not seem to be commonly understood in the UK that the French grading system considers the overall difficulty of the climb, taking into account the difficulty of the moves and the length of climb. This differs from most grading systems such as the British technical grade where a pitch or single pitch route is rated according to the most difficult section (or single move). In the French system grades are numerical, starting at 1 (very easy) and are open-ended. In this guide book, consistent with common practice, routes of F5 or under may be sub-divided with + or – while routes graded 6 and above are subdivided by adding a letter (a, b or c) and + or – may be used to further differentiate difficulty.

Grades throughout are believed to be accurate and where possible this has been based on independent feedback. The same applies to route quality ratings. As always they are subjective and no doubt will give rise to some healthy debate – part of the richness of climbing. Feedback on any issues is welcome: mjdoyle1@yahoo.com.

Eco bolt, Petzl with stainless steel hanger and a marine grade stainless steel bolt.

Bolts

A mixture of bolts have been used throughout the area, the type used being largely dependent on when the particular venue was developed and who was doing the work. These include 'glue-ins' (DMM, Fixe and staples) and 'through expansion bolts' with hangers (Fixe and Petzl). Both systems have advantages and disadvantages in installation but hangers are less kind to karabiners in actual use and cannot be used to lower off from directly. The glue-ins have been fixed with either dual component resin from cartridges or, more recently, spin-in self-contained resin capsules. Both methods are well proven. Stainless steel glue-in bolts and hangers have been used throughout. It has been noted that some of the studs securing the hangers on a very few older routes have a discoloured look to them. This may be surface corrosion or even just discolouration but should be treated with caution. Hangers fixed with stainless steel bolts (as at **The Gallery**) have lasted extremely well.

Some lower-offs are already showing signs of wear, especially where they are shared by more than one route. Even stainless steel wears. Replacing bolts costs money and climbing time and is largely avoidable. Please, therefore, use your own quickdraws for lowering off as much as possible (last person threads) to minimise wear. The number of bolts on a route (where known) has been identified throughout (see: Using the guide).

Equipment

A 50m single rope will suffice at all locations other than **The Gallery** and **Notice Board Crag** when 60m is essential for some routes. Ten quickdraws will, almost always, be more than sufficient; however, as many as 15 may occasionally be needed at **The Gallery**. In addition, it is wise to carry a couple of screwgate karabiners and a narrow sling. Wearing a helmet is very desirable, not only because of the risk from stone fall but also to avoid injury as a result of turning upside down in a fall.

Groups & top roping

Easily accessible lower grade sport climbs such as those at **Penmaen Head** and **Castle Inn** often attract groups from outdoor centres and groups of beginners. Unfortunately, this often leads to the monopolisation of certain routes as a line of people wait to try a route on a top rope. It also means that those routes are likely to become polished far more quickly than otherwise and, if your own quickdraws are not used, that the lower-offs

will wear more quickly and need replacing. This can be unreasonable. The problem of beginner groups being top-roped on some of the sport climbs in this guide while wearing mountain or walking boots is also an issue. This is an inappropriate practice on sport routes and can quickly lead to damage and polishing. If beginners are at a stage where they are wearing big boots then there are plenty of alternatives on trad crags with Diffs and V. Diffs which are far more suitable for this activity without affecting established sport routes.

Please be aware of the needs of others; remove ropes that are not in use and avoid popular climbs at busy times. Fortunately, the selfish continental practice of leaving ropes and quickdraws in place on a route while going off to try another route or to have lunch has not yet taken hold in Britain. The wear and tear that climbs are suffering is a growing problem. If you must visit the crags in a large group, please consider other climbers and try to avoid monopolising classic climbs which are likely to get the most traffic anyway

Chris Doyle on the first ascent of Fathers for Justice (F6c) Expressway Wall, Penmaen Head 21.04.08. Photo Michael Doyle.

Access & conservation

(Provided by the BMC Cymru access officer)

Many of the climbing sites along the A55, especially the limestone cliffs, are designated as Sites of Special Scientific Interest on account of the flora and fauna that is found on the calcareous grasslands that are associated with the limestone outcrops along this part of the North Wales coast. The designations give legal protection to these sites, which include **Castle Inn** and **Llanddulas Cave**, and climbers need to be aware that gardening and cleaning activities at these sites could be deemed illegal under the Wildlife & Countryside Act. Climbers are asked to be sensible and discreet in opening new routes in these areas, and to take account of the special features and vegetation on these cliffs.

The cliffs (and in particular caves on the cliffs) are the breeding and roosting sites for bats, which also have very strong legal protection. If you come across bats in crevices on the rocks, avoid disturbing them and give them a wide berth. If disturbed during the hibernating season they would probably die from the cold very quickly. If you do encounter any access problems, then please do not antagonise the landowner or other organisations, but refer the issue to the British Mountaineering Council's Access & Conservation officers at the BMC Wales office (☎ 01690 720124) or the Manchester office (☎ 0161 445 6111).

The BMC Regional Access Database is an excellent resource for up-to-date crag access information; www.thebmc.co.uk/bmccrag

> All land is owned by somebody and the inclusion of a venue in this guide does not imply that you have a right to go there. There are no known access issues at any of the venues in this guide but climbers have an obvious vested interest in acting responsibly. This includes responsible parking, taking your litter home (and other people's), respecting Sites of Special Scientific Interest (SSSIs) and generally keeping a low profile.

📷 *Mynydd Marian Nature Reserve, home to the Silver Studded Blue Butterfly (below).*

Photo iStockphoto.com

SANITATION

We all have to 'go' somewhere – but please try to 'go' before going climbing. Toilet paper and faeces are all too common at continental sports crags, an unsightly health hazard which is sure to upset landowners. Most of the venues in this guidebook are close to villages and towns where there are public toilets. Please try to use them rather than the nearest tree or boulder!

PARKING ISSUES

Many access problems are caused by parking, especially at sites that suddenly become popular due to redevelopment works. Always park considerately; avoid blocking gateways and driveways, or causing an obstruction. This is especially important for groups using minibuses or larger vehicles. Wherever possible, try to share transport to minimise parking problems and also reduce your carbon footprint (it's also cheaper if your mate pays for the fuel).

North Wales Bolt Fund

Many thanks are due to Chris Parkin who administers the North Wales Bolt Fund and who was always quick to help out when requested with gear for the redevelopment of **Llanddulas Cave**, **Penmaenbach Quarry** and **The Gallery**. A contribution to the NWBF will be made from any profits from this guide. The NWBF relies on donations from the climbing community and companies associated with climbing. Bolts cost money and stainless bolts a lot more. Drills, resin and static ropes all eat away at the donations so it needs constantly topping up. If you have enjoyed the routes in this guide (or even if you haven't!) then please consider making a donation to the North Wales Bolt Fund and support your sport.

Donations can be sent to: NWBF, Llysfaen, Lon Brynteg, Glyn Garth, Menai Bridge LL59 5NU or collected at: V12 – Llanberis, Joe Browns – Llanberis & Capel, Great Arête – Bangor, The Beacon Climbing Wall and The Indy Climbing Wall. Cheques should be made out to: North Wales Bolt Fund.

CLIMBING IS POTENTIALLY DANGEROUS

You might die or be very seriously injured. In all cases you are responsible for the decisions you make and your own judgement and no responsibility can be accepted for the way you use this guide. Rock can break and bolts, although extremely unlikely, have been known to come out. The route descriptions and grades are given in good faith and believed to be as accurate as possible but essentially it is your judgement which counts. It is a very bad idea to climb unless you have had previous instruction and are fully familiar with the techniques and equipment used.

The author, publisher and distributors of this book do not recognise any liability for injury or damage caused to, or by, climbers, third parties, or property arising from such persons seeking reliance on this guidebook for their own safety.

📷 *Lower-off chains installed at Castle Inn crag.*
Photo Pete Wood.

Glyn Davidson on the first ascent
of Adolescent Stimuli 01.09.09.
Photo Michael Doyle.

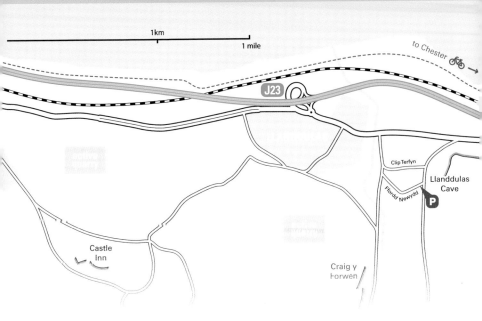

LLANDDULAS CAVE

An all-weather venue with the Upper Cave now having four sport routes inside, three of which may remain dry in all but the wettest weather, adding considerably to the lure of the place. After an extensive makeover in 2008 and 2009 involving new routing, much rebolting of established routes and removal of loose rock and vegetation, Llanddulas Cave is now pretty much fully developed with a set of excellent sport routes, some up to 22m in length.

There are two areas; the **Forgotten Sun** area which faces north-west and the **Upper Cave** area which faces north. The cave at the **Forgotten Sun** area to the right of *Field of Dreams* is home to two boulder problems. The **Forgotten Sun** area gets the sun from about mid-afternoon and the **Upper Cave** much later, which makes it a pleasant venue in hot weather. **Llanddulas Cave** tends to be very sheltered when other nearby destinations are windy, rainy or blisteringly hot. Its sheltered nature and the steepness of the rock means that most of the crag rarely holds water and vast parts of it seem to escape the rain altogether (although flat holds, ledges and the start of some routes can get wet). With the adjacent caves to shelter in, it makes an excellent destination in showery weather when other areas are wet. The **Forgotten Sun** area does not entirely live up to its name and can be very pleasant with the sun starting to filter through the trees in the mid to late afternoon. There is one obvious area of seepage that never dries up but little seepage elsewhere unless there has been sustained heavy rain.

Dan Wellings on Poet Lariat (F6a) 'Forgotten Sun Area.' Photo Michael Doyle.

ACCESS RESTRICTIONS

The area is within an SSSI (Gwrych Castle wood) but there are no known access problems. The left side is also mapped as open access land under the Countryside and Rights of Way Act (CROW Act), which allows access on foot for walking and climbing.

APPROACH

From the east or west: Leave the A55 at Llanddulas (Junction 23). Turn left at the roundabout by the filling station. Drive through the village and as you come out turn right immediately before the village hall (Beulah Avenue). Take the second left (Ffordd Newydd – New Road) and park responsibly at the top of this road. Take a left at the end of New Road. After 50 metres and just past the junction with Clipterfyn, go through an obvious break in the wall on the right and up a footpath into the woods. Trend left and the **Forgotten Sun** area is soon revealed on the right. For the **Upper Cave** area stay on the main footpath and take an obvious footpath up to the right after a short time.

Upper Cave

Forgotten Sun

P

Forgotten Sun Area

This is the first area reached from the access path and is mainly quarried rock. *Field of Dreams* starts just to the left of the cave where the access path reaches the crag. To the left there is a permanent seepage line and *Udder Head* starts immediately to the right of this. Left to right, the first route starts 2m right of the grotty vegetated groove.

1 White Man's Burden ★   🌐 F6b+

FA C. Struthers, S. Siddiqui 11.96

Previously incorrectly named 'White Honkey' and now rebolted with resin bolts (07.09). Clips the first couple of bolts of *Ralarwdins* then moves left to cover some steep, rough rock and rejoins *Ralarwdins* at the lower off. Start at some easy stepped rock.

2 Ralarwdins ★★★   🌐 F6b+

FA M. Griffiths 1995

A superb route up an obvious line which gets steeper and more technical the higher you get – and in perfect safety. What more could you want? Start at some easy stepped rock.

3 Stretcharmstrong ★   🌐 15m F6c+

FA M. Griffiths 1995

Good climbing to a hard and very steep finish. Start just left of the wet streak then trend left to a small corner.

4 Tho Man with the India-rubber Head ★   🌐 15m F6a

FA T. Taylor 1995

Shares the start and the first couple of bolts with *Stretcharmstrong*. Enjoyable and steady at the grade, but not easy to work out sometimes. Go right at the third bolt. Start just left of the wet seepage streak.

5 Udder Head ★   🌐 15m F6a

FA T. Taylor 1995

More good climbing. Gain the ledge and finish up the leftwards leaning groove to the same lower-off as the previous route. Start just right of the wet streak.

6 Name of the Pose ★   🌐 15m F6a+

FA T. Taylor 1995

Another worthwhile route in the same genre as the previous two. Now with an independent start and an extra bolt to access the cleaned ledge. Steepish to a slightly puzzling finish. Start below a rock scar.

7 Clipterfyn   🌐 15m F5+

FA I. Andrews, M. Doyle 29.05.09

A harder move past the first bolt gains access to the ledge and easier climbing above. Start just left of the cracked pillar below the first bolt and climb direct to the ledge.

8 Poet Lariat ⑤ 15m F6a

FA M. Doyle 02.05.09

Climbed on the day the new poet laureate was appointed. Gain the jutting ledge and climb up left of the third bolt to finish steeply slightly right. Start below the white streaks.

9 Not Runout Groove ★ ⑤ 15m F5+

FA M. Doyle, M. Lally 02.06.09

A variation on *Runout Groove* at a more consistent grade. Clip the first bolt of *Field of Dreams* and move left in the concave bay to clip a second bolt and mantle the ledge. After clipping the third bolt above, step right easily to gain the bottom of the groove and follow this to the lower-off.

10 Runout Groove ⑤ F6b

FA at E3 5c: K. Jones 1991

The original but very uneven. Clip the first three bolts of 11 then continue up the obvious groove to the lower-off.

11 Field of Dreams ★ ⑤ F6b+

FA N. Clacher 20.04.91

A good pitch with a cruxy move to a poorly positioned second bolt leading to the ledge. The upper wall offers further tricky climbing. Purists may want to know that the cleaned ledge to the left of the second bolt was not part of the original route and use of it makes the route easier. Start immediately left of the cave entrance.

There are two boulder problems within the cave between *Field of Dreams* and *Prime the Pump*. On the left wall: *The Portcullis V6* (J. Bertalot 08.09) takes a traverse line of undercut flutings, leading to a cool roof covered in mini-stalactites. Start at the cave entrance, traverse in on the flakes and get established on the roof (crux). Cross this rightwards and finish matched on a sloping shelf on the right. Only the holds you'll need have been cleaned and the friction is good. A tad esoteric and a head-torch may help! The problem on the opposite wall starts low at the cave entrance and traverses left using the undercut flutings at about V3.

12 Construction of Meaning ⑤ F7a

FA: Pre 1997, retro-bolted: T. Shelmerdine, M. Burrows

Start as for *Field of Dreams*, traverse right above the cave then up the seemingly blank wall.

13 Crack of Dawn ★ ⑤ F6b

FA N. Clacher, T. Shelmerdine 12.03.09

Described as "Definitely uphill" by one ascentionist. Steep climbing with enjoyable moves on some good holds (a shame there's not more of it). Start at the left end of the scooped cave by the tree.

14 Gone Down Under   (hangers removed) F7b
FA P. Smith 05.95

This route has not been re-equipped as it seems rather a pointless variation. Climb the centre of the shallow, scooped cave and move out left to climb the very steep wall. Start as for Prime the Pump in the centre of the scooped cave.

15 Prime the Pump ★★   F7b
FA M. Griffiths 05.95

Climbs steeply up the centre of the scooped cave to a water-worn niche with harder climbing to gain the upper wall. Start in the centre of the shallow scooped cave.

16 Pump Action   F7a
FA P. Hawkins 1998, rebolted 08.09 M. Doyle, L. Proctor

Climb the overhanging right side of the scooped cave after which a brief respite can be had where it meets *Trail of the Snail*. Suitably rested, tackle the short but steep, compact headwall with the crux at the top. Hangers and glue-ins. Start at the right-hand side of the scooped cave and finish on ledges at a chain lower-off.

17 Trail of the Snail ★   F6b
FA N. Clacher 11.05.91

Newly rebolted with resin bolts and uses *Prime the Pump* lower-off. Clip the first two bolts of *Forgotten Sun* then traverse left. Start as for *Forgotten Sun.*

18 Forgotten Sun   F6b+
FA N. Clacher 11.05.91

Updated with a more realistic grade and an extra bolt installed at the start. Start just round the corner from the scooped cave.

19 A Brief History of Lime   F6c
FA T. Shelmerdine 1995

A leftwards-trending line. Start right of *Forgotten Sun.*

20 Duckworth Lewis   F6b+
FA N.Clacher, T. Shelmerdine 11.03.09

Takes in two overlaps and a hard move from good starting holds. Start just left of the cave mouth.

21 Milo   F6b
FA N. Clacher, T. Shelmerdine 08.06.09

A nice hold for the left-hand allows a move to more good holds. Pull over the overhang to the steep wall. Start at the cave mouth.

The Upper Cave Area

The path exits at the large cave. As far as limestone goes, the rock to the right and left of the cave is quite different. The routes left of the big cave are variations on a theme and on steep rock that was vegetated and neglected for many years and has long deserved a makeover. It was prone to looseness but hopefully the loose rock has all now been removed on the routes which have steep, vertical faulting with holds that aren't always obvious.

The whiteness is caused by lichen which doesn't pose a problem but the routes can sometimes feel rather dusty. They should settle down with traffic, however. The routes right of the cave are on white, compact limestone reminiscent of the Ormes and featuring a number of pockets. The last three routes start on the slope below the ledge of *P.C. Wimpout*. The starts of those routes are fairly easy, up stepped rock but give the routes logical lines and lead to much steeper climbing.

① Karmic Wind ★   🔂 17m F6a+

FA P. Hawkins 1995, cleaned and rebolted: M. Burrows 07.08

A climb which feels a tad sustained. It's the first climb just right of the vegetated rock.

② Mind Light ★   🔂 18m F6a+

FA M. Burrows, T. Shelmerdine 13.08.08

A sister route to *Karmic Wind* and mainly on good holds. Takes the shallow rightwards-trending groove to a crack and then chain lower-off. Start 1m right of *Karmic Wind*.

③ Spider Mite   🔂 18m F6b

FA T. Shelmerdine. Ria Roberts 08.08

Harder in the lower part but relents as you get higher. Now with two extra bolts as the first ascentionist wasn't keen on the finishing run-out! Start 3m right of *Mind Light* just left of a small keyhole-shaped grotto.

④ Llanddulas Ditchwater   F6c

FA C. Struthers, S. Siddiqui 1999

The name is a pun. Petzl hangers with a bolt belay. Start at some holes just left of a shallow depression. No lower-off.

⑤ Early Bird   E3 5c

FA D. Lyon, D. Summerfield 01.07.84

Climb to a groove above the holes leading to a wide crack. Currently loose and needs cleaning. Start just left of the cave entrance at some holes.

Inside the cave:

⑥ Main Overhang   A2

FA Unknown

Grotty and ill-equipped aid climbing with rotting gear although a recent ascent was noted. Not recommended.

8,9 & 10

El Tigre.
Photo Michael Doyle.

Route 7 is a F8? project *(Equipped by C. Doyle 09.09.09)* following the line of an ancient aid route starting from the left-hand wall and takes the big roof towards the right-hand wall. It then finishes up *Zoidberg*.

The next four routes are inside the cave on the right-hand side on rock that should remain permanently sheltered from rain (except route 9). However, the starts can be greasy in damp conditions possibly due to condensation. Chain lower-offs for routes 8,9,10.

8 Guano on Sight ★★　　　　🔗 13m F6a+

FA T. Hodgson, S. Chesslett, I. Jones at E2 5c 29.06.84, retro-bolted: M. Doyle 01.09.09

A well-bolted route providing an enjoyable excursion up the bulging tufa feature. It will undoubtedly get a lot of traffic and become a classic. Climb the bulging tufa and, at the fourth bolt, a harder move is forced before moving left to easier ground. Start just right of the tufa.

9 Adolescent Stimuli ★　　　　🔗 13m F6b

FA G. Davidson, M. Doyle 01.09.09

A reference to the cave as a popular drinking venue for kids evidenced by the regular empty can and bottle debris. Some satisfying moves. At the third bolt find a good hold in the scrape and make a stiff pull to wobble up into it. Start right of the first bolt and step left along the break underneath the tentative tufa.

10 Rosalind Franklin's Picture 51　　🔗 13m F5

FA M. Doyle, C. Doyle 10.09.09

The line to the left of the gully is worthwhile and straightforward if it's dry. It becomes very much harder in low light and damp conditions as the foot placements are difficult to see and it can be greasy (anywhere between F5 and F6a). Start in the gully but quickly leave it by bridging on the opposing walls. At the top don't forget to admire the view out of the hole before lowering off.

11 Zoidberg　　　　　　　　　🔗 15m F6c

FA T. Shelmerdine 01.09.09

'Zoidberg' is a cartoon, mutant lobster and the obvious name for this particular route. It takes a line up shallow holes on the wall opposite routes *Adolescent Stimuli* and *Rosalind Franklin's Picture 51* and uses some good holds to link a couple of much harder sections together. Start in the gully and bridge across the opposing walls up to the second bolt where good holds allow a pull onto the upper wall and a short traverse right. Now the fun starts. Make a hard and strenuous reach using a good pocket. Another long reach gains easier ground and the lower-off.

Out of the cave the first two routes to the right (for those with sufficient talent and strength) should also remain dry in nearly all conditions.

12 The Wirral Whip ★ F7c+

FA M. Collins 11.86, rebolted L. Proctor 08.09

Thin, strenuous and technical but now more friendly with some extra bolts. Start below the right-hand tufa, just right of the cave entrance.

13 Mudjekeewis ★★ F7b+

FA P. Hawkins 1995

The name means 'west wind' in a native American language as it was very cold at the time of the first ascent. A crimpy route which finishes up the short arête to the right of The Wirral Whip. Start 1m right of the tufa pillar.

14 Pearl from the Shell ★★ F6c+

FA T. Hodgeson, S. Chesslet 27.06.84

Intricate pocket pulling to the ledge then move up from the fourth bolt to a crack to finish at a twin bolt lower-off. Start at some small holes below a vague groove.

15 Sticky Fingers ★★ F7b+

FA T. Shelmerdine 1996

Takes the middle of the overhanging wall above the ledge and shares a lower-off with *Pearl from the Shell*. Trend right to the scoop then launch into the overhanging prow. Start as for *Pearl from the Shell*.

16 Searching ★ F6c+

FA T. Hodgeson, S. Chesslet, P. Custy 27.06.84

Good climbing and now with an extra bolt to finish. It features a high first bolt which is relatively easy to reach and has a sting in the tail. Start at the left end of the cleaned ledge.

17 El Tigre ★ F7b

FA P. Hawkins 1998, newly bolted version T. Chamings, K. Chamings 14.08.08

A good line offering thin and technical climbing with a powerful but easier finish over the bulge. The crux moves are between the first and second bolts. Named after Tony 'the Tiger' Shelmerdine. Start on the ledge at the low belay bolt.

18 P.C. Wimpout ★ F6b

FA at E2 5c T. Hodgeson, S. Chesslet, P. Custy 27.6.84, retro-bolted: T. Shelmerdine, N. Clacher, M. Burrows 07.08

Lovely climbing initially on sharp pockets and deceptively steep. Start from the right-hand end of the cleaned ledge.

The next three routes start on the slope below the ledge of *P.C. Wimpout* and behind a large tree. Left to right:

19 Grog and the Donkey * F6b+

FA T. Shelmerdine, N. Clacher 09.08

Excellent, steep and sustained climbing up the white stuff above the ledge by the second bolt and reachy in parts. Deal with the scrappy start and from the ledge pull left using cracks. Then climb elegantly upwards. Spaced bolts.

20 Afterglow * F6a+

FA at E2 5c T. Hodgeson, S. Chesslet, P. Custy 27.6.84, retro-bolted: T. Shelmerdine, N. Clacher, M. Burrows 08.08

A decent climb which originally started on the ledge above. Surprisingly good after the broken start and can seem much harder if the correct sequence in the upper section isn't found.

21 Turtle Tripler F6b

FA R. Roberts, T. Shelmerdine 01.06.09

The right-hand route has a steeper start than the previous two routes. Head up broken rock heading for just left of the obvious block and then a shallow, well-bolted groove in which unhelpful holds briefly make it harder.

Ian Andrews on the first ascent of Clipterfyn (F5+) Forgotten Sun Area. Photo Michael Doyle.

Mike Burrows on Route 2 (F6a) Castle Inn.
Photo Michael Doyle.

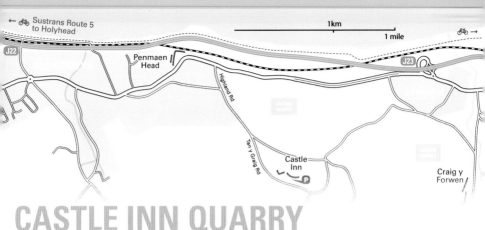

CASTLE INN QUARRY

Surely the definitive convenience crag! A crag in the car park of a pub (now sadly closed) with tarmac almost up to the first holds. It's not just highly convenient but it also has a selection of very fine routes on some lovely flowstone along with nice views across the valley. A recent addition is the development of Fine View Wall 50 metres to the left (if you can stomach the walk-in) which offers more quality climbing and a mix of sport and trad routes.

A south facing, quick drying and sunny crag which can be exposed to the wind.

ACCESS RESTRICTIONS

None. However, the area is within an SSSI and the local Mynydd Marian nature reserve. The car park under the crag is apparently the property of the local authority. The ground beneath the left-hand buttress (**Fine View Wall**) is important as a breeding ground for the Silver Studded Blue Butterfly, a nationally rare species. Care should be taken not to disturb the semi-natural grassland in this area, or to leave gardened vegetation or rock lying on the grassland. This particular butterfly has an interesting life cycle that relies on a symbiotic relationship with the black ant which carries the butterfly larvae to their nest. The larvae then feeds on secretions from the ants. That's enough about secretions from ants for now.

APPROACH

From the east (Chester): Come off the A55 expressway at Llanddulas (Junction 23). Turn right at the roundabout by the filling station and then immediately left towards Old Colwyn (A547). Follow the road for one mile to just before the crest of the hill. Turn left up Highlands Road and after 0.4 mile fork right into Tan y Craig Road (between the two limestone walls). After another 0.4 miles turn left into the car park at the old Castle Inn. From the west (Llandudno): Come off the A55 expressway at Old Colwyn (Junction 22). Turn right under the expressway and turn left at the roundabout soon after towards Llanddulas/Abergele (A547). After about 1.5 miles and after a crest in the hill, turn right up Highlands Road and after 0.4 miles fork right into Tan y Craig Road (between the two limestone walls). After another 0.4 miles turn left into the car park at the old Castle Inn. The routes are described from left to right.

Chris Doyle on the first ascent
of The Walking Furnace (E3 5c)
Fine View Wall. Photo Michael Doyle

1 Mogadishu · F4+

FA R. Roberts, T. Shelmerdine 03.05.08

The first route right of the vegetation starts up some stepped rock and then goes more steeply right to the lower-off.

2 More Than This · F6a

FA M. Burrows, M. Doyle 16.06.08

Clip the first two bolts of Mogadishu if need be and then move right into the short groove. From the last bolt pull round the arête to finish up the slab at the lower-off for *The Outsider.*

3 The Outsider · F6c

FA M. Delafield 1991

Thin climbing on the slab to the left of the *Finale* crack and using the same bolts.

4 Finale · F5

FA C. Goodey 1991

The obvious crack provides a pleasant enough climb.

5 School Mam ★★ · 24m F6a

FA at E3 (original line) G. Gibson 20.05.84

The modern and more logical way (thanks to an extra bolt at the start) to do this route is to access the ledges left of the tree and climb the crack at the left of the bolts. The original started up Cakewalk Direct and went technically, diagonally left to reach the main line at an unbalanced 6b.

6 Cakewalk Direct ★★ · 24m F6c

FA T. Shelmerdine, A. Barnett 03.02.93

Climb the steep slab and make a stiff pull through the roof to finish. Start just right of the tree.

7 The Cakewalk ★★ · 24m F6b+

FA unknown, finish climbed at E3 by A. Pollitt, T. Hodgson 31.08.82

The slab above the recess gives some thin, technical moves and leads to a right-facing corner at the top. Start just left of the overhanging recess.

8 Route 3 ★★★ ⑦ 23m F6c
FA at E3 A. Pollitt, T. Hodgson 31.08.82, top-roped by C. Goodey and friends in 1959

A super route! Steep climbing up the crack is followed by contrasting sustained, thin and technical stuff up the white-streaked slab. Start just right of the recess.

9 Route 2 ★★ ⑦ 25m F6a
FA at E2 C. Goodey, A. Davies 1959

Another fine, slabby pitch which heads up over the overlap and with a slightly technical move in the middle.

10 Route 1 ★★ ④ 25m F5
FA at HVS C. Goodey, A. Davies 1959

A very good route which climbs the arête mainly on the left on some great flowstone features. Run-out but with straightforward climbing to finish. Start from a ledge at the base of the arête and either come in from the right or tackle the arête direct.

11 Cross Winds ★ ❸ F6c
FA R. Davies 30.06.90

To the right of *Route 1* is a short route.

12 Driving the Dumper ❷ F6c
FA A. Pollitt, T. Hogdeson 31.08.82

A direct line and rather run out to the same lower-offs as *Cross Winds*. Start as for *Cross Winds* but go right over two overlaps.

13 Solid 6 ❷ F7a
FA W. Wayman, F. Crook 08.10.83

Contrived. Clip the first bolt above the notched overlap and move up diagonally left to the second bolt on *Driving the Dumper* to finish up this. Start below the notch in the overlap.

📷 *Gareth Buckley on School Mam (F6a) Castle Inn. Photo Pete Wood.*

14 Fuel Injected ⓷ F7b+

FA R. Davies 11.05.91

The description in the 1997 Rockfax guide can hardly be improved upon: 'A hideous boulder problem with three bolts and one nightmare section'. That's enough off-putting quotes for now. Start to the left of a small corner if you can.

15 Secret Garden ★ ⓸ F6c

FA N. Jowett 12.88

Make for the second bolt on the white and pink flowstone veneer and pull over the overlap to trend diagonally right to the lower-off. Start on the first rock step up the gully below an upper groove.

16 Green Fingers ⓷ F6b

FA L. Davies 28.09.90

Climb the short groove to a small overhang and then up to a narrow ledge. Shares a lower-off with *Secret Garden*. Start further up the gully at a ledge.

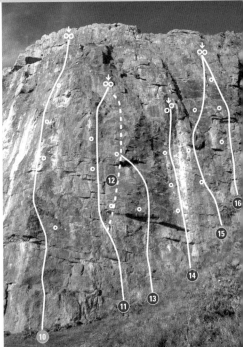

There are a couple of routes on the next area of clean rock a few metres to the right of the main crag and are worth doing if only as warm-ups. These constitute the final new routes at **Castle Inn** – until the next final new routes anyway. They are essentially independent lines but share the last two bolts before the lower-off.

17 Conan the Libertarian ⓸ 12m F6a

FA M. Doyle, M. Lally 22.10.09

The left hand line makes the most of the clean rock on the slender, slabby wall and avoids nearly all of the arête. Start between the two dirty cracks to the left of the broken corner.

18 October Premiere ⓸ 12m F5+

FA M. Lally, M. Burrows 22.10.09

The name is a reference to Miss Lally's first new route. The right-hand route joins up the cracks on the right-hand side of the slabby wall. Start up the dirty crack immediately to the left of the broken corner.

Chris Estabrook on Mogadishu (F4+) Castle Inn. Photo Pete Wood.

Margaret Lally on
Indian Summer (F6a)
Fine View Wall.
Photo Michael Doyle.

Fine View Wall

This fine wall of excellent rough rock is obvious 50 metres to the left of **Castle Inn** main crag. It faces east and dries quickly.

It has been climbed on for many years, probably as early as the 1960s, as evidenced by the old stakes, peg and bolt on top. However, despite the obvious quality of the climbing, it had never become popular. Possibly because the routes have never featured in a guidebook. It had become clear that most of the routes had been climbed and then repeatedly claimed as first ascents over the years and renamed accordingly. It has not been possible to establish who the first ascentionists were, nevertheless, credit should go to them. Most of the routes offered here are therefore merely the latest versions.

In June of 2008, with the development of **Penmaen Head** substantially complete, it was decided to give this crag a makeover and it was duly named **Fine View Wall**. Bolts were installed at the top to supplement the stakes and the cracks were cleaned of clay and loose rock. The starting ledges were cleared of turf.

Belay at the top for all routes. Note that while the wall itself tends to be a sun trap, it can be exposed and chilly on top when belaying. Add 3m to the route lengths to reach belay bolts/stakes. From left to right the routes are:

① Indian Summer ★★   ⊕ 15m F6a
FA M. Doyle, M. Burrows 20.09.08

Just right of the arête. Great climbing on clean and extremely rough rock. Finish directly above the last bolt. No use of the arête now for this tick! Superbly superb.

② Mynydd Marian ★★   14m VS 4c
FA unknown

The obvious crack line to the right of *Indian Summer* offers a good route.

③ As You Like It ★★   ⊕ 13m F6b+
FA M. Burrows, M. Doyle 10.10.08

The next sport route and very agreeable climbing on clean, rough rock which leads to the detached shield. Move right and right again to gain the headwall where steep moves on crimps allow a wobble up left and a long reach to finish. Well bolted.

④ Pioneer Cracks ★★   ⊕ 13m E1 5b
FA unknown

The wide crack. Climb up to the top of the corner (excellent wire placement) and over the overlap to finish steeply. Good climbing and well protected.

⑤ The Walking Furnace ★   12m E3 5c
FA C. Doyle, M. Doyle 20. 09. 08

Start up the bank below a diagonal slot. Climb up to the slot and a good cam placement. Thin moves right and up lead to the corner crack and another good cam placement. Fix further gear in the corner crack before launching out over the overlap and up the steep headwall.

Chris Doyle on the first ascent of The Double Helix (F6a+) 14.03.07. Photo Michael Doyle.

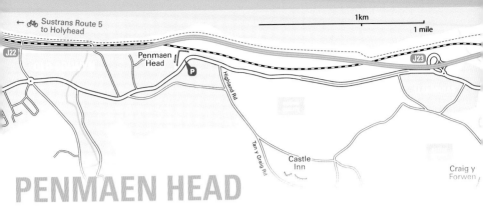

PENMAEN HEAD

A recently developed venue on the headland above Old Colwyn and just off the A55. It offers fifty-seven sport routes and one trad route, almost all good quality and well bolted with easy access and a flat base to start. Even on the shorter routes the climbing tends to be very absorbing. The seven sectors are quite distinctive in character according to the nature of the rock which demands slightly different styles of climbing.

The place was known as Penmaenrhos Quarry and the quarrymen have apparently done the climbing community a favour in the way it has been developed. Serendipitously, the quarrying progressed along vertical fault lines to reveal a number of natural faces which provide very good climbing on excellent natural rock There are routes between F5 and F7a+ but the vast majority of routes are in the F6s, thereby providing an excellent venue for the lower and mid-grade sport climber. Bearing in mind the quality and quantity of the climbing and ease of access, it is astonishing that it wasn't discovered from a climbing development point of view until October 2006. This is especially so as the wonderful **Expressway Wall** is so obvious from the A55 and must have been glanced at by thousands of climbers over the years as they returned from the Ormes and Snowdonia.
Almost all loose rock that can be removed has been removed and most routes have been cleaned with the intention of providing quality final products. The "stuck-on holds" (mainly **Penmaenrhos** and **Flowstone Walls**)

are actually quite sound and have had some heavy use. They also give some of the routes their character. The occasional red patches of rock tend to be brittle and rather snappy and should be treated with caution. All routes have two lower-offs and most have lower-offs in the form of steel karabiners. These have been nipped closed and require to be threaded. It is hoped to equip all routes in this way eventually. There is some traffic noise from the expressway, particularly when at **Expressway Wall**, but this is quickly forgotten when climbing. The maximum length of routes is 20 metres.
Feedback on grades and route quality has been received from various people since the complex has been under development (many thanks to all who have contributed) and the grades of some routes modified accordingly. Route grades seem to have settled down of late. After feedback a number of extra bolts have been installed. Please take your litter home and treat the place with respect but, above all, enjoy the climbing.

Norman Clacher on That's Enough New
Routes for Now (F6c) Expressway Wall.
Photo Michael Doyle.

The crag faces south-west and gets the sun just after 1.30 p.m. in the summer and slightly later in the winter. This makes it a good venue for morning climbing in hot summers or, in the winter, afternoon climbing, when it can become a sun trap. It can be particularly pleasant on sunny evenings and remarkably sheltered when a northerly wind is blowing.

The complex tends to dry quickly after rain and a lot of the steeper routes can substantially escape rain altogether. The bottom of the middle of **Penmaenrhos Wall** seems to remain permanently dry. Some routes are subject to sustained seepage after heavy rain, particularly in the area where the left-hand end of **Penmaenrhos Wall** meets the right-hand end of **Flowstone Wall**. An odd patch on **Wen Wall** and **Expressway Wall** is also subject to seepage after rain.

ACCESS RESTRICTIONS

It is not clear who currently owns the quarry as the land has not been registered with the land registry. It was owned by a major quarrying company called Kneeshaw Lupton but, after an application to open a quarry near the Isle of Harris in 1965, the trail goes cold. It is unclear whether they went out of business or were assimilated by another company. The stepped part of the footpath from the top lay-by is a public footpath. There have been no access problems to date but the climbing community has a vested interest in maintaining this trend by acting responsibly, keeping noise down and keeping the place litter free. The quarry was used as a general rubbish dump which was cleared up as the place was developed. There has been some vandalism in the past to garden fences adjoining the path and to the steps. These then had to be closed as persons unknown had spent a lot of energy prising out a number of the huge limestone steps. Big fun for tiny minds. The path was closed and the damage repaired by the council. It is hoped that the presence of climbers will discourage such behaviour in the future.

APPROACH

From the east (Chester): Come off the A55 expressway at Llanddulas (Junction 23). Turn right at the roundabout by the filling station (great bacon baps at the '55 Diner' by the way) and then immediately left towards Old Colwyn (A547). Follow the hill for 1.5 miles to just over the crest of the hill where a lay-by for limited parking can be seen on the right by the apartment development known as Cliff Tops. From the west (Llandudno): Come off the A55 expressway at Old Colwyn (Junction 22). Turn right under the expressway and soon turn left at the roundabout towards Llanddulas/Abergele (A547). After about one mile and almost at the crest of the hill, park in the lay-by on the left. Follow the steps down the public footpath from the lay-by and the crag quickly appears on your right. The sectors are listed right to left as you go down the steps from the lay-by.

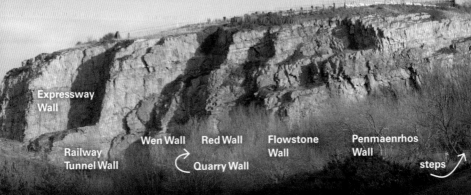

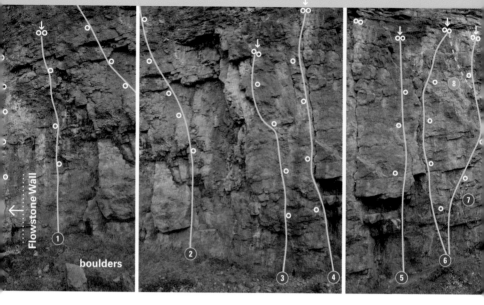

Flowstone Wall

boulders

← Flowstone Wall

① ② ③ ④ ⑤ ⑥ ⑦ ⑧

Penmaenrhos Wall

This sector is characterised by steep climbing on rock which was a tad dusty and had some loose rock. It seems to have settled down with traffic and the climbing is now relatively clean. It has a couple of rare crack lines. To reach route 1 walk down the path in front of the sector to two prominent boulders. The boulders mark the start of **Penmaenrhos Wall** and are to the right of the obvious flutings of *Flowstone Shuffle* which is the last route on **Flowstone Wall**. From left to right the routes are:

① Barney Rubble ★ ⊕ 12m F6b+
FA N. Clacher, M. Burrows, F. Gowling 21.07.08

Aptly named! Beware of the rubble stuck on with clay in the upper part of the route. The belayer may want to stand to one side. Nevertheless, it offers some good, steep climbing with the crux over the overlap. Start 1m left of the grotty corner and behind the two obvious boulders.

② Whilst You Were Away ⊕ 16m F6b+
FA D. Kells, C. Struthers 17.07.08

A right to left diagonal line over some crozzly rock and up a shallow corner to the overlaps. Through bolts/hangers. Start at the corner at the right side of the block.

③ Discomknockerated ★ ⊕ 11m F6b+
FA N. Clacher, I. Andrews 01.05.08

Takes the impending wall left of the obvious crack line. Start below the small overhang. Make steep moves up the wall using some surprising stuck-on holds, moving left at a stuck-on ear to easier climbing.

④ Flaschenburste Crack ★★ ⊕ 12m F6a
FA N. Clacher, I. Andrews 28.04.08

Good climbing up the left, wider crack to a pumpy crux. Start in the corner below the crack. Named after a washing-up brush from Lidl used for brushing holds.

⑤ Ambergis ⊕ 11m F6b+
FA N. Clacher, I. Andrews 06.05.08

The wall right of the wide crack lacks independence. Start below the low stepped overhangs.

⑥ Helyg Crack ★ ⊕ 12m F6a
FA N. Clacher, I. Andrews 28.04.08

More good climbing up the right-hand crack. Move right before the lower-off. Start steeply just to the right of the crack.

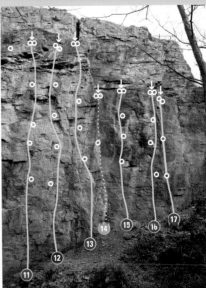

7 Desiderata   ⚡ 12m F6c

FA N. Clacher, I. Andrews 25.06.08

A strenuous number which uses one of the hangers on *Red Handed*. Start steeply and make a hard move right to the undercling. A long reach is then needed to latch a poor crimp before moving leftish up the ramp. Start 2m right of *Helyg Crack* at a small overlap.

8 Red Handed   ⚡ 12m F5+

FA C. Struthers, D. Kells 17.07.08

A right to left rising traverse protected by through bolts/hangers. Not very good. Start at a broken inverted corner.

9 Intruder ★   ⚡ 12m F5+

FA C. Struthers, P. Evans, K. Stephens 13.07.00

Some nice wall climbing on great holds in the upper half. A low first bolt. Start at a crack below the obvious ledge.

10 The Trouble with Girls ★★   ⚡ 12m F6b+

FA N. Clacher, T. Shelmerdine 17.07.08

A very high and rather reachy first bolt with an undercut move to gain the steep upper wall. It just keeps coming and the difficulties seem to be much longer than they actually are. Start below the stepped ledges.

11 Sir Crimpalot   ⚡ 12m F7a+

FA T. Shelmerdine, M. Burrows 26.07.08

The steep, crimpy wall and the hardest route at Penmaen Head. Start 1m right of *The Trouble with Girls*.

12 Top Secret ★★   ⚡ 11m F6c

FA N. Clacher, I. Andrews 07.02.08

A fine route up a slight leftwards leaning corner and with some long reaches. It lacks some independence from *Terces Pot*. Start 3m left of arête.

13 Terces Pot ★★   ⚡ 11m F6c

FA N. Clacher, I. Andrews 19.02.08

Another good route which starts just left of arête and is best climbed near the arête to maintain independence from the previous route.

14 Broken Blackbird   ⚡ 8m F5

FA N. Clacher, I. Andrews 01.02.08

The arête yields a poor climb. Start at the foot of the arête.

15 Scared Shipless ★   9m F6a+

FA N. Clacher, I. Andrews 01.02.08

Technical moves past the first bolt lead to easier climbing.
Start in the middle of the wall at some reasonable holds.

16 Another One Bites the Dust   9m F6c

FA N. Clacher, I. Andrews 19.02.08

Climb the steep wall just left of the arête to the second
bolt and be prepared for testing moves past it to a jug on
the arête where it relents. Start just left of arête.

17 Steak Slice   9m F5

FA I. Andrews, N. Clacher 01.02.08

The obvious corner is pleasant enough.
Start at the bottom of the corner.

Flowstone Wall

The sector above the limestone pavement. Properly
cleaned and with some great flowstone climbing and
'stuck-on holds'. Note that the flowstone veneer on
Dead Moggy Syndrome and *Go with the Flow* is soft
under the thin, outer skin and only an inch thick. Some
of these routes share lower-offs: routes 1, 2, 3; routes
6, 7; routes 8, 9. From left to right the routes are:

1 Richard II 1399 ★★   11m F6a

FA M. Doyle, C. Doyle 10.03.07

Enjoyable climbing with convenient holds where
needed. Tip: a middle digit may be useful. Use of
the arête diminishes both the difficulty and quality
of the route so trend right under the first bolt and no
use of the arête for this tick! Start at the flowstone
depression just right of the arête.

2 Big up the Lizard ★   11m F5+

FA C. Doyle, M. Doyle 10.03.07

Worthwhile. Start below the first bolt at a
slight depression.

3 Tan y Lan Kids ★   11m F5

FA M. Doyle, C. Doyle 10.03.07

The first sport route at Penmaen Head and pleasant
climbing through the crozzly stuff. Start 1m right of
Big up the Lizard.

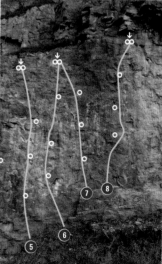
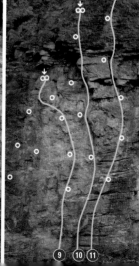

4 The Burning Spinster ★ 🔗 11m F6b

FA M. Doyle, C. Doyle 14.03.07

Harder and quite thin at the start since a hold broke off making the first bolt a much more difficult clip. Start by stepping up from the right end of the flat block.

5 Dead Moggy Syndrome ★★ 🔗 11m F6b

FA C. Doyle, M. Doyle 14.03.07, direct finish climbed in error by John Eames 14.09.08 (original route finished diagonally right)

Absorbing stuff left of the three bolts and finishing direct up the left side of the shallow groove with a long reach above the first bolt. Start below an obvious horizontal slot.

6 Go with the Flow ★★ 🔗 11m F6a

FA I. Andrews, N. Clacher 01.05.08

An agreeable route up the flowstone veneer which quite delights the senses. Start at a rock step below the undercut handhold.

7 The Double Helix ★★ 🔗 11m F6a+

FA C. Doyle, M. Doyle 14.03.07

Can be puzzling at the grade but has some pleasing moves and good climbing. Start at the left end of the ledge.

8 Statement of Twilight Years ★★ 🔗 11m F6b

FA M. Doyle, C. Doyle 20.08.07

A rather reachy climb moving right of the first bolt. Start from the right-hand end of the ledge.

9 Fixe Inox City ★ 🔗 11m F6b+

FA C. Doyle, M. Doyle 20.08.07

Engaging moves up to clipping the turned bolt and more testing fare to finish. Start on the earthy ramp below a high roof.

10 Aphelion ★ 🔗 14m F6a

FA I. Andrews, F. Gowling 05.07.08

Takes the big detached flake and launches out over the overhang on good holds. Start at a shallow groove below the big flake.

11 Blitzy's Jug ★★ 🔗 15m F6a+

FA M. Doyle, M. Burrows 09.02.08

An excellent and varied route with a bit of everything. Climbs the wall to the right of *Aphelion* on stuck-on holds to the crack. Climb this and then wobble up over the overlap (crux). Keep something in reserve for the steep, crimpy finishing moves on the wall above.

12 Flowstone Shuffle ★★★ 🔗 11m F6b+

FA C. Doyle, M. Doyle 20.08.07

A classic and deservedly popular. Takes the impending wall and flutings on some good holds (if you can find them among the choice). Easier after the last bolt to the lower-off.

13 Swing Time for Hitler 🔗 F6a

FA F. Gowling, Ian (Hitler) Rowell 05.05.08

A rising traverse right starting as for route 1. Clip the first bolt of *Richard II 1399*, then the second bolt of the next route, the third bolt of the next route and finish at the lower-off of route 4 *The Burning Spinster*.

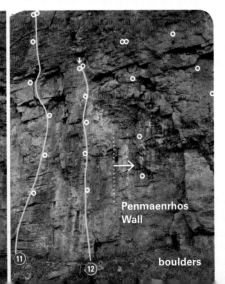

Penmaenrhos Wall

boulders

11

12

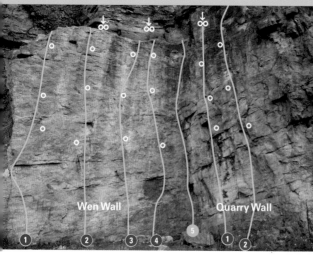
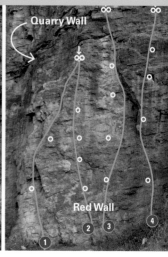

Red Wall

Some strenuous climbing on rock similar to that of **Penmaenrhos Wall**. It is the red triangular crag to the left of **Flowstone Wall**. From left to right the routes are:

1 Calling all Wimps   🔩 11m F6a

The arête with the groove. Take a few medium nuts to supplement the bolts and pull steeply into the groove on good holds. Start just right of the arête.
FA N. Clacher solo 29.02.08

2 The Green Bus ★   🔩 11m F6c

FA N. Clacher, I. Andrews 02.03.08

Named after a toy green bus which was glued to the rocky plinth (since vandalised). Start at the rocky plinth.

3 Criminal Bay ★   🔩 13m F6c

FA N. Clacher, I. Andrews 28.02.08

Difficult moves off the rocky plinth lead right to steep and strenuous bridging up the leftwards leaning corner.

4 Grandad's Jumper   🔩 13m F6b

FA T. Shelmerdine, N. Clacher 11.03.08

Takes the line to the right of *Criminal Bay*. A poke in the butt with a sharp stick aided the first ascent. Start just left of the broken corner.

Quarry Wall

To the left of **Red Wall** and at right angles to it are a couple of lines on quarried rock. From left to right the routes are:

1 Ying   🔩 9m F6a+

FA I. Andrews, N. Clacher 29.02.08

The left-hand line.

2 Yang   🔩 10m F6a+

FA I. Andrews, F. Gowling 28.04.08

The right-hand line.

Wen Wall

The small white wall immediately to the left of **Quarry Wall** offers some exquisite climbing with two sets of lower-offs accessed from the ledge. From left to right the routes are:

1 Gabrielle's Arête ★   🔩 10m F6a

FA M. Burrows, M. Doyle 12.11.07

Gain the sharp block on the arête and then step right on to the wall to climb this. Start just right of the arête.

2 Charlotte's Goal ★★   10m F6c+

FA M. Burrows, M. Doyle 25.10.07

Technical climbing makes this rather difficult. Before the third bolt was installed, the original route trended diagonally left at 6c from the second clip. Using poor layaways, poor crimps and good technique finish direct. Start 1m right of the arête.

3 Jenny's Welsh Cap ★★   10m F6b+

FA M. Doyle, M. Burrows 12.11.07

Nice wall climbing which may seem harder if you don't find the crucial crimp. Named after the first ascentionist's daughter who had just got a Welsh woman's rugby cap. Start 1m right of *Charlottes Goal* below the third line of bolts.

1 Tunnel Vision   11m F6a

FA I. Andrews, M. Doyle 14.03.08

A pleasant route. Start 3m right of the arête. Top out up the bank and use a sling on an iron spike at the bottom of Expressway Wall to lower off.

2 Pier Pressure – £10 down   11m F6a+

FA F. Gowling, M. Doyle 17.04.08

Good climbing to a tricky finish slightly left. Start below the large stuck-on plaque. Top out up the bank and use a sling on an iron spike at the bottom of Expressway Wall to lower off.

3 Retirement Day ★   11m F6a

FA M. Doyle, I. Andrews 14.03.08

Steep climbing which trends diagonally right and finishes just right of the obvious rocky boss. Climbed on the day the first ascentionist retired. Start below the right end of the large stuck-on plaque. Top out and use a long sling over a substantial piece of iron just over the lip to lower off.

4 Snowdrop ★★   10m F6a+

FA R. Roberts, T. Shelmerdine 15.02.08

A good route which gets progressively steeper and more crimpy. Start at the large flake.

4 Hammy's World Tour ★★   10m F6a

FA M. Doyle, M. Burrows 25.10.07

Good climbing at the grade. Named after Hazel Findlay who was starting out on a world cragging tour at the time. Start 1m left of the corner.

5 Chris Corner ★   Severe 10m

FA P. White, C. Darlington 1975

Yes, it's trad! Takes the obvious corner crack. Start below the crack.

Railway Tunnel Wall

To the left of **Wen Wall, Railway Tunnel Wall** has some nice flowstone climbing and proves to be surprisingly steep. From left to right the routes are:

5 70 Degrees ★★   19m F6c

FA N. Clacher, T. Shelmerdine 23.02.08

Easier climbing left of the flake leads to the upper wall which provides more intricate fare. The line wanders around a bit in an attempt to maintain a consistent grade and can feel rather bold. From the fourth bolt, move right to below the overlap, up and left again to clip the next bolt. Start at the flake.

6 Clogau Gold ★★   🔂 21m F7a

FA N. Clacher, T. Shelmerdine 16.03.08

Climb the broken crack to the ledge where a rest can be had while contemplating embarking on the steep upper wall through the overlap. Start below the broken crack.

A worthwhile variant was established by Tommy Chamings and Norman Clacher in summer 2008. This gives a very pumpy 7a+ which incorporates the crux moves of the last two routes and gives a full 25m pitch with a really exposed feel. Climb *70 Degrees* and, after the fourth bolt, traverse to the undercut arch by the third bolt on *Clogau Gold*. The traverse is very run out and it's a bit spicy clipping the bolt above the arch. There is also a low level V3 traverse below these routes *(O. Rees 17.04.08)*

Expressway Wall

Above **Railway Tunnel Wall** and accessed via ledges from the left. This sector offers fine, open and highly absorbing climbing on rough limestone. The odd patch of red rock is soft and can be rather snappy.

These routes share lower-offs: routes 1, 2; routes 6, 7; routes 8, 9. Routes 8, 9; and routes 10, 11; also share the same start. From left to right they are:

1 The Long Run Home   🔂 12m F6a

FA M. Doyle, M. Burrows 31.03.08

Move left to the arête and better holds after the second bolt. Start 2m right of the arête at the low bolt.

2 That's Enough New Routes for Now ★🔂 12m F6c

FA C. Doyle, M. Doyle 01.05.08

The main difficulties are concentrated between the second and third bolts. Move up just left of the second bolt. Going right was the original way at about 7a. Start 1m right of *The Long Run Home*.

3 Fathers for Justice ★★★   🔂 16m F6c

FA C. Doyle, M. Doyle 21.04.08

A nicely pumpy number with some elegant (hopefully) moves. After clipping the third bolt step down and span left from a good hold to an indistinct quartzy ramp and finish right of the final bolt. Start in a shallow groove.

4 The Quarrywoman ★★★   🔂 17m F6b+

FA M. Doyle, M. Lally 30.06.08

The prow direct. Quality climbing throughout to the lower-off.

5 Hotel 70 Degrees ★   🔂 17m F6b

FA M. Doyle, C. Doyle 21.04.08

A bit squashed in but some worthwhile climbing nonetheless. Head for some layaway moves before the break and finish just right of the prow on a slab. Start just left of a red patch of rock.

6 Clwyd M.C. *   🔗 17m F6a+
FA M. Doyle, M. Burrows 16.04.08

Up to small groove where a longish reach leads to easier climbing. Start at the left-hand iron spike.

7 Ryan's Route *   🔗 17m F6a+
FA I. Andrews, M. Doyle 09.04.08

The vague central groove gives another treat. Start at the left-hand iron spike.

8 Kneeshaw Lupton **   🔗 16m F6c+
FA C. Doyle, M. Doyle 01.05.08

Shares the start of *The Mankind Initiative*, the first three bolts of which lead to an upper section which proves to be much thinner and more technical. Move up left of the fourth bolt and finish up the little groove. Start just right of the right-hand iron spike.

9 The Mankind Initiative **   🔗 16m F6b+
FA M. Doyle, M. Burrows 24.04.08

A contrasting route where balancy climbing leads to a bulge where a hidden pocket allows access to excitingly steep finishing moves involving the crack. Trend diagonally right from the third bolt. Start just right of the right-hand iron spike.

10 Paranoia Crack **   🔗 17m F6b
FA M. Doyle, M. Lally 22.04.08

Reflects the paranoia which creeps in when new routing and there are first ascents outstanding! Takes a rightwards trending line to climb the contrasting obvious upper groove and crack. At the break step right into the bottom of the steep groove which proves to be somewhat strenuous. Start on the shelf by the grotty corner at some reddish rock.

🖼 *Norman Clacher on his own route 70 Degrees (F6c) Railway Tunnel Wall. Photo Michael Doyle.*

11 Adams Exams *   🔗 18m F6a+
FA M. Burrows, M. Doyle 02.05.08

As for *Paranoia Crack* to the grotty corner then take the fine, right-hand crack line up lovely, rough rock. Another cracker. Start at the grotty corner at some reddish rock.

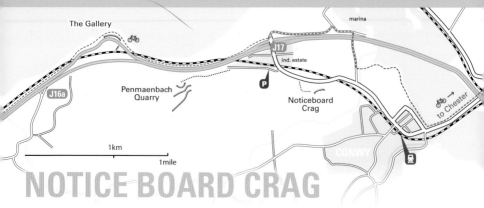

NOTICE BOARD CRAG

The rather daunting, very steep and imposing crag high up on the slopes of Conwy Mountain (*Mynydd y Dref*) above the A55 and just before the Conwy tunnel, with some impressive routes on mountain rhyolite.

The notice board has (at the time of writing) disappeared leaving only the pole. This was possibly due to an appalling spelling mistake on the board which for years proudly proclaimed: 'Danger: Sheep Drop'. It should, of course, have warned: 'Danger: Sheep Droppings'. Sadly neglected in recent years, frankly the crag could do with a makeover. Strictly speaking, with only one sport route, it is not a sport climbing crag. The rock is generally very solid and pocketed, flinty in nature with sharp holds. Faded threads and rusty pegs are in place but they are obviously very old and the integrity of these should not be relied upon. Bolts are rusty and the same applies. The pole at the top which supported the notice, together with a number of nearby belay stakes, can be used for belaying (well back). The routes have only been visually checked and the descriptions are based on those in the 1997 Rockfax North Wales Limestone guide with the permission of Alan James. It is hoped that the inclusion of the crag in this guide will provoke some interest in giving it the makeover it deserves. Check the resource: northwaleslimestone.wetpaint.com for this and updated information about all the crags in this guide.
The crag faces north-west. Being high the crag dries quickly but is also exposed to the wind.

ACCESS RESTRICTIONS

The cliff is on land that is mapped as open access under the CROW Act and the land is owned by Conwy County Borough Council who manage it as part of Conwy Mountain – Countryside Site.

APPROACH

Come off the A55 at Junction 17 just west of the Conwy tunnel. Turn right if coming from the west and left if coming from the east (the A 547) towards Conwy. Drive over the A55 and the railway bridge and then immediately turn right and park about 100 metres or so down this road (a dead end and the old A55). Double back and head towards Conwy for about 300 metres to cross a stile on the right and head up the hillside towards the crag. There are two possible approaches to the exposed ledges below the crag: Head towards the base and make a dodgy but short, grassy scramble up to the ledges or continue to the top of the crag and down the other side to a fence at a notch. Slither down a short crack to substantial grass ledges and belay bolts. The routes from left to right are:

the pole

The old notice.

DIBYN SERTH

PERYGL

DANGER

SHEEP DROP

① Go Zone   14m E3 5C

FA R. Deane 19.05.88

Start by a bolt at the left-hand end of the ledge. Climb up to a thread then move right. Step right to a peg and move back left and up to the top. Belay on block.

② Born Again   25m E5 6b

FA P. Hawkins 02.88

Start below the clean wall before the drop down. Climb the wall past a thread to a peg then move right to a shallow cave. Pull right over the bulge and finish direct.

③ Leaning Jowler   25m E2 5b

FA S. Howe 02.88

The central line gives excellent climbing. Start by a low bolt and thread. Climb grooves (bolts) to a niche. Traverse right to join the top of *Fiendish Beanish*.

④ Fiendish Beanish   28m F7b

FA G. Smith 02.88

Superb pocket pulling up the right-hand side of the wall. Start from the lower section of the ledge (high first bolt) or slide in craftily from the higher ledge. Continue up the sustained wall above to the top. Rusty bolts.

📷 *Gareth Buckley on Káto (F5+)
Penmaenbach Quarry. Photo Pete Wood.*

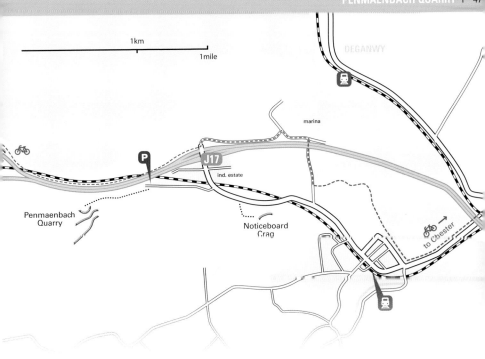

PENMAENBACH QUARRY

Penmaenbach operated as a quarry from 1873 until the 1940s and this rather enigmatic venue now offers some worthwhile, quality routes across the grades on compact rock with good friction. This includes a small but fine slab in the lower quarry and some hard and much longer slabby routes in the upper quarry.

The rock is a very hard diorite, about five times harder than limestone (which becomes immediately clear if you try to drill it). While the friction is good, the compact nature of the rock can be disconcerting. The **Lower Quarry** was subject to a makeover in late 2009 courtesy of Mike Doyle and Mike Burrows and the many rusty bolts were replaced with stainless steel glue-ins. Extra bolts have been installed at the start of some routes (due to very high first bolts) and ledges have been cleared of loose rock and turf. Additionally, lower-offs have also been installed for most routes. Most of the routes in the **Lower Quarry** were developed by Arthur and John Bowman in 1991. At the time the defeat of Wales at the Cardiff National Stadium by the unfancied Western *Samoa* (16 – 13) was a *National Disaster* for Wales. Information on these routes was received late in production so the area is absent from the histories at the back of the book.

Simon Moore on Rambling Jack (F6b)
Penmaenbach Quarry. Photo Pete Wood.

The **Upper Quarry** consists of a small triangular slab on the left with one well-bolted route. To the right and behind is a large slab with four big routes. A further slabby wall exists 100 metres to the right with one route. Some routes in the **Upper Quarry** could do with a makeover due to rusty bolts and single bolt lower-offs. There are fine views towards the Great Orme and, surprisingly, no traffic noise from the A55 below. The quarries are north-west facing. One might expect that the lower quarry may be sheltered due to its recessed nature but the wind does seem to swirl around in there sometimes. The sun only reaches the **Lower Quarry** in the evening but earlier in the **Upper Quarry**, which is a lot more exposed. The lower half of the **Lower Quarry** is subject to seepage after rain and most of it can be subject to run-off from the top after heavy rain. The **Upper Quarry** dries quickly but sometimes has a streak of seepage to the left of *Slab Tony Chamonix*.

ACCESS RESTRICTIONS

There are no restrictions. The land is owned by Conwy County Borough Council who manage it as part of Conwy Mountain – Countryside Site.

APPROACH

Come off the A55 at Junction 17 just west of the Conwy tunnel. Turn right if coming from the west and left if coming from the east. Drive over the A55 and the railway bridge. Then, immediately where the road bends left, turn right and drive to the end of the road (a dead end and the old A55). Park in a lay-by at the end, just before the gate. Cross the stile into a quarry and head right along the path, gently rising on a good path through bracken and gorse up the hillside to an incline, aiming for the obvious old winding house on the ridge. The track levels off at the winding house so keep on this level to reach the **Lower Quarry** after a few metres. The **Upper Quarry** can be reached by going up the next incline to the next level. Fifteen minutes from the parking.

Winding house · Upper Quarry · winding house · Lower Quarry · A55 Expressway

The Lower Quarry

Recessed and vaguely square cut, the **Lower Quarry** has a slabby wall on the left wing with one route and a central section which looks more broken but has some good climbs. These are surprisingly balancy and technical on solid, compact rock. The right wing has a clean and rough slab which sports another couple of short but fine routes. There are stakes for belaying or fixing lower-off slings for the routes on the wings but twin bolt lower-offs have been installed for the other routes. Most of the first bolts were very high so extra bolts have been installed at the start.

THE LEFT WING

① Kato   ⚂ F5+

FA D. Lyon, C. Stevenson 2001

A climb which takes the short but worthwhile clean upper wall on the left wing. Easy up to clipping the second bolt. Belay stakes are at the top but take a couple of long slings to lower-off from. Start at the bottom of a ramp.

THE CENTRAL SECTION

② The Poor Route   ⚄ F6b+

FA J. Bowman, M. Forbes 1991

Start on the slab and step left to clip the first bolt following the rib. Very unbalanced in grade with easy climbing between the bolts, a hard finishing move and a high first bolt. It hardly seems worth re-equipping. There are two hangers to lower-off but no karabiners. Rusty bolts. (Originally named Catalan.)

③ Rambling Jack ★   ⚄ F6b

FA A. Bowman, J. Bowman 1991

A nice line on compact rock up the wide but shallow, square-cut slot. Trend left after the first bolt. Start in the small corner with the bore hole. New lower-offs.

④ Hitachi Arête ★★   ⚂ F6a+

FA J. Bowman, A. Bowman 1991

Balancy climbing up the rib just to the right of the square cut slot. Start at a small V groove 2m right of *Rambling Jack*. New lower-offs.

⑤ Tricky Dickie ★★   ⚃ F7a

FA D. Lyon, C. Stevenson 2001

The fine open-book groove above the ledge isn't quite as blank as it looks but still gives technical and thin bridging for those with the flexibility, and the start is no pushover either. Start in a broken corner until it is possible to pull left onto the ledge beneath the groove. Loins suitably girded, head upwards. New lower-offs.

⑥ National Disaster   ⚃ F6a

FA J. Bowman, A. Bowman 1991

The rib to the right of *Tricky Dickie* is quite technical for the grade. New lower-offs.

THE RIGHT WING

The fine slab to the right has excellent friction. The two variations share a common start and a finish on stakes at the lip, so take a couple of short slings to lower-off.

7 Samoa *   1 peg + 2 F8a

FA J. Bowman, A. Bowman 1991

Takes a line to the left of the bolts. From the bottom of the rib on the right climb up to the high peg. Step left and up the slab. Using the crack to the left before clipping the second bolt is a cop-out and diminishes the quality.

8 Playboys **   1 peg + 2 F6a+

FA A. Bowman, J. Bowman 1991

A short but involving route. Using the same start as *Samoa* climb directly up the slab to stand on the obvious central blister. Move up and reach left to a positive horizontal rail rock-over and then finish direct.

The Upper Quarry

The main event at the **Upper Quarry** is the obvious and impressive slab which has four routes up which *Slab Tony Chamonix* drives an improbable line. It is only truly a slab on the left where *The Birdman of Minffordd* goes and the lines to the right are up much steeper rock which qualifies as a slabby wall. A hundred metres to the right is another area of solid, black streaked rock which is home to another bolted route (6b+?) about which not much more is known. The routes have only been visually checked with feedback from the first ascentionists in the main. A 60m rope is recommended for routes on the **Main Slab**.

To the left of the **Main Slab** there is a small diamond-shaped slabby wall which has a line of bolts on its right-hand side. There you will find *Wiser (FA R. Hughes 1999)* 6b+, three rusty bolts with a one bolt lower-off.

There is a further slabby wall 100m to the right of the **Main Slab** which sports another route with four bolts. There is further scope for new routes on this wall. No further details are available.

belay on trees

krab

krab

📷 *Gemma Simone on National Disaster (F6a) Penmaenbach Lower Quarry. Photo Pete Wood.*

THE MAIN SLAB

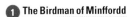 1 The Birdman of Minffordd   🔟 F6c

FA D. Lyon, C. Stevenson 2001

Makes the most of joining up lines of weakness up the left slab and finishes up the steep headwall to belay on trees. From the low belay bolt, aim diagonally left towards some broken rock. A blank section then beckons through a couple of tiny overlaps to a small groove. The bolts then lead right to finish up the headwall. Start at a belay bolt at the left side of the black streaks. Stainless steel bolts.

2 The Gruffalo   🔩 F6c+

FA D. Lyon, C. Stevenson 2001

A route up the black streaks to a single bolt (hanger) lower-off. The hanger currently sports a karabiner but the integrity of this is not verified. It may be advisable to carry a sacrificial krab. Stainless steel bolts.

3 Slab Tony Chamonix   🔩 F8a

FA N. Dyer 2004

A sustained and technical route up the faintest of grooves to the right of the black streaks involving poor smears and some wacky lay-backs to a lower-off where the angle eases. From the ground it is not clear how any upward progress can be made up the compact rock beyond the high first bolt, but the route has had at least three ascents to date. It may be advisable to carry a sacrificial krab. Rusty bolts. Originally a Tony Shelmerdine project, hence the name.

4 The Shouting Stage ★   40m E5 6a

FA F. Ball 1991

A good route which was previously incorrectly recorded as 'The Shooting Stage'. It follows the right leaning, thin crack and broken ground which marks the right edge of the slab, passing a couple of pegs. Then move up and left past old twin bolts, crux, to reach the base of a shallow, bottomless corner with a peg. Follow the corner to a bulge which is taken slightly left, passing another peg to finish. The route could do with a makeover and replacement of the old gear.

Steve Long on *This Land is Your Land,*
Gallery Lower Crag. Photo Colin Struthers.

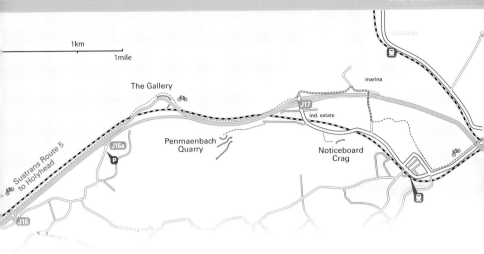

THE GALLERY

An accessible crag of microdiorite which has excellent friction and the crag has many overlaps. On first acquaintance it looks rather loose and intimidating but is actually quite solid. The style of climbing is characterised by the profusion of technical lay-away and side-pull moves which demand subtlety and technique as the moves are very often not obvious. One climber used to 'boning down' on very hard and steep, crimpy limestone found himself getting spanked on supposedly much easier fare at The Gallery!

Some holds are reassuringly sharp but the downside is they can also be rather painful. The council has laid down a surface of climber-friendly (presumably unintended) stone chippings immediately below the main crag making an ideal base to launch upwards from. Part of the crag is quarried. The main crag is at Penmaen-bach Point, known locally as 'Violet's Leap' and is on the seaward side of the A55 Penmaenbach tunnels. The brooding, very black **Upper Crag** is impressively perched high up above the easterly A55 carriageway tunnel exit.

The route descriptions below are largely based on Nadim Siddique's original topo (with permission) and have been updated as required with recent developments and recent feedback. Most routes are well bolted and the extra investment in stainless steel bolts by the original developers has paid off as the gear seems to have lasted extremely well to date. As a few routes require a 60m rope, it is prudent to take one (and tie a knot in the end) for all climbing at **The Gallery**, so that there are no issues regarding running out of rope when lowering off. As many as 15 quickdraws (includes two for the lower-offs) are occasionally required for the longer routes. Some obvious sharp edges have been blunted but beware of the rope running over well-defined corners and sharp edges, particularly on the routes at the right of the crag. Taking some long quickdraws to prevent this is a good idea.

Gallery M. Hounslea on
Infantile Disorder (F6c+).
Photo Kevin Stephens.

Lower-offs were originally mainly hangers fitted with karabiners but the karabiners are well past their best. A recent campaign by Colin Struthers and friends of replacing them with hangers and rings has taken place and this is indicated in the text where necessary. At the time of writing this process had not been completed but it should be long finished by the time the guide is published. Check the resource: northwaleslimestone.wetpaint.com/ for up-to-date information.

The main crag is north-west facing and the upper crag is north facing. **The Gallery** faces the sea, dries quickly and can be very pleasant in the evening sunshine. The main crag gets the sun obliquely from late afternoon and doesn't seem to suffer from much seepage. It does get runoff from the top after prolonged rain but the left end seems to escape even this. It is exposed to westerly winds. The **Upper Crag** is exposed and dries quickly.

ACCESS RESTRICTIONS

The Gallery main crag is above a public cycle and walk way and there are no known access restrictions. Because of the location adjacent to the A55 expressway, the presence of climbers might draw the attention of highway officers. If approached be polite and refer them to the BMC's access team. It appears that the **Upper Crag** is on land that is mapped as open access land under the CROW Act. Be aware of cyclists and walkers on the track below the crag. Historically, the **Upper Crag** was a site of peregrines nesting but this does not appear to have happened for some years. However, this could change so please take note of any signs to that effect and any temporary climbing restrictions.

APPROACH

From the east (Chester, Llandudno): Exit the Penmaenbach tunnel and after 0.5 mile come off the A55 at Junction 16a (signposted Dwygyfylchi). Park just beyond the gate and cattle grid after about 100 metres.

From the west (Bangor): Come off the A55 at Junction 16 (signposted Penmaenmawr/Dwygyfylchi) and immediately turn left to Dwygyfylchi. Stay on this winding road for one mile until the A55 can be seen again and park on the right just before the gate and cattle grid.

To reach the crag (10 minutes) from the parking, walk to the A55 and cross carefully (it's like a race track). There is a vague path which crosses the central reservation and on the other side of the road is the cycle and pedestrian walkway. On reaching this, turn right towards the tunnels and the impressive lower crag appears.

Upper Crag

Lower Crag

seaside block

cycle way

Lower Crag

Left to right the routes are:

1 On a Swing and a Prayer ★   F6b+

FA K. Stephens, N. Siddiqui, C. Struthers 07.08.99

The first route takes the prominent slab up left to a corner and the name describes the crux which is a puzzling move to reach the large jug at the lip. Once solved, use this jug to go left to the much easier upper slab. New lower-offs.

2 Infantile Disorder ★★   ⑥ F6c+

FA C. Struthers, N. Siddiqui 06.98

Up the slab to the overhanging flake and use this to reach surprising holds and hence gain the upper slab. To finish, head up to the left set of lower-offs (oddly vertically placed). Start 3m right of the previous route at quarried rock. New lower-offs.

3 Nil by Mouth ★   22m F6c+

FA N. Siddiqui, C. Struthers, R. Siddiqui 18.09.98

Climb the slab, pull right through the overlap then climb up steeply and step back left to gain the upper slab. The route now has an independent direct finish and new lower-offs have been installed. Start at undercut rock 3m right of the previous route.

4 Language, Truth and Logic ★   F7a+

FA N. Siddiqui, C. Struthers, N. Colton 29.07.99

A steep and technical direct route. Start at the left end of a grey slab.

5 Stagger Lee ★   F7a

FA C. Struthers, N. Siddiqui 02.07.99

Pass an apparently solid detached block left of the bush and weaving up the overlaps, finish at a short corner. Start at the right end of the grey slab below the bush.

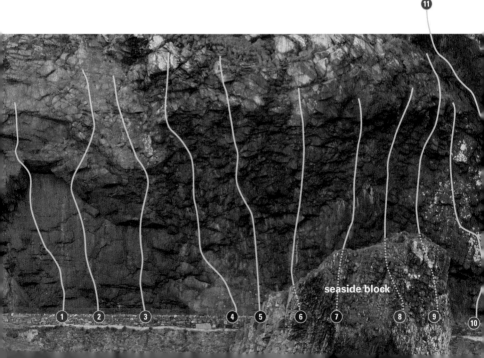

seaside block

6 Intimate Strangers *   F7a

FA C. Struthers, N. Siddiqui, G. Harrison 05.10.98

Climbs powerfully, directly up the wall passing a protruding fin at the left of the triangular slab and faint groove. Gain the left-hand side of a small slab at the top. Start just left of a white circle around two drilled holes. New lower-offs.

7 Renaissance Man **   F7a+

FA C. Struthers, N. Siddiqui 29.07.99

From undercuts at the top of the obvious triangular slab launch up and slightly right of the bolts before moving back left to more undercuts. Clip the lower-off easily then relax to elegantly lay back the fin on the left. Start at a white streak just right of the painted white circle around two drilled holes.

8 Fever Pitch *   F6c+

FA N. Siddiqui, C. Struthers 25.07.99

Another fine route which gains the right end of the undercut slab and finishes up the right leaning flying groove. Start below a small slabby bay.

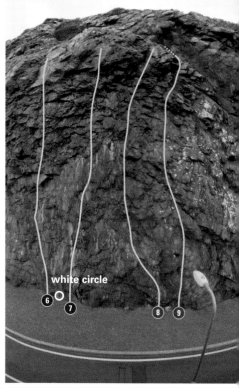

white circle

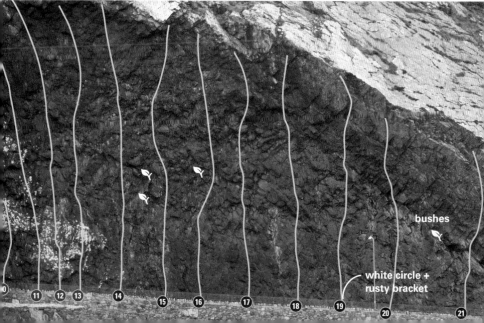

bushes

white circle + rusty bracket

9 Swiss Tony   F6b

FA C. Struthers, N. Siddiqui 09.05.99

Start up the hanging rib and then work up to a niche in the roof to finish directly. Start at a downward pointing fang opposite the lamp post. New lower-offs.

10 Criminals of Want   F6b+

FA N. Siddiqui, C. Struthers 09.05.99

Aim for a small left-facing corner and finish directly. Start just right of the slab and roof and 3m right of *Swiss Tony*. New lower-offs.

11 The View Belongs to Everyone ★★   30m F6b

FA C. Struthers, N. Siddiqui 09.05.99

Rather spectacular and now with three extra bolts, it feels very well protected. Up the slab moving left and back right to gain a prominent slab next to a left-facing corner groove and then a chimney up which the route finishes. Named after a song by Fun Loving Criminals. Start under the left end of the lower slab with the white lichen circles. 60m rope essential. New lower-offs.

12 This Land is Your Land ★★★   F6c

FA C. Struthers, N. Siddiqui 25.07.99

Mr Struthers favourite route at **The Gallery** so it must be three star! Climb directly up the slab with the white lichen circles to an arête which leads to a large ledge. Finish through the notch in the roof above. The last bolt before the ledge is on the left side of the arête and the bolt above the roof is on the main fin and hidden from below. Start 2m right of the previous route behind a drain inspection cover. 60m rope essential.

13 Free the Forwyn ★   F6c+

FA C. Struthers, N. Siddiqui 16.05.99

Climb directly to the ledge, then up slightly left to a bolt. Continue through bulges to gain the upper left-leaning groove. Finish up a weakness to the right of the jutting overhang. Start 1m right of the previous route.

14 You Can Do Magic ★   F7a+

FA N. Siddiqui, C. Struthers 18.07.99

A very direct route to the lower-off taking a line to the left of a bush. Start 2m right of the previous route.

15 Put a Spell on You ★★   F7a

FA N. Siddiqui, C. Struthers 04.04.99

Passes a large projecting block at 8m on its right-hand side and climbs between the bushes. Trend slightly left and climb a shallow left-facing corner, moving right to a lower-off below the roof. Superbly sustained. Start at broken rock below the obvious jutting block.

16 Truly, Madly, Steeply ★   F7b

FA N. Siddiqui, J. Burton, C. Struthers, R. Siddiqui 11.10.98

Heads up to the right of the bush. Gain a niche at 10m. Move up left and climb the bulging wall directly. Start below the obvious right-hand bush.

17 Finnegan's Wake   F7a+

FA C. Struthers, N. Siddiqui 18.07.99

Climbs to a central depression then up a steep groove to a hands-off rest. The move past the last bolt is difficult. Named after the impenetrable book by James Joyce as, with the book, the route is hard to read. Start 3m right of the previous route.

> The next routes climb up to the leftwards-rising diagonal fault and then tackle the very steep head wall.

18 The Evil that Men Do ★   F7b

FA N. Siddiqui, C. Struthers, K. Stephens 19.08.99

Climb up to an overlap and through this to difficult moves right over a bulge. Undercut moves then lead left to a finale up the overhanging corner. Start below the prominent corner above the rising fault.

19 Rock Savage   F7b+

FA N. Siddiqui, C. Struthers, N. Colton, K. Stephens
& R. Siddiqui 05.09.99

Climb to a hands-off knee jam below a bulge. Hard lay-
away moves lead to a flat hold on the left. Move up past
the bolt to small holds on a ramp, then move right to good
holds and strenuously back left to finishing lay-back moves.
Start at a white circle painted around a rusty bracket.

20 Ourselves Alone   F7a+

FA C. Struthers, N. Siddiqui

Climb up to jams and an old peg at the rising diagonal
fault. Hard and strenuous step-ups lead to overhanging
finishing moves. *Ourselves Alone* (a translation of *Sinn
Fein*) – a route done towards the end of the development
when their mates had departed, having had quite enough
of drilling holes and holding ropes. Start 2m right of the
rusty bracket and white circle. New lower-offs.

21 Violet s Leap *   F7a+

FA D. Kells, C. Struthers 10.10.2009

A steep line through the overlap with both technical and
strenuous moves to a double clip lower-off.

📷 *Kevin Stephens climbing Nil by Mouth*
(F6c+) Gallery Lower Crag. Photo P. Evans.

Upper Crag

Follow the cycleway/pedestrian walkway further east beyond the tunnel exit for about 100m to where there is a grassy bank on the other side with a retaining wall above it. Wait for a lull in the traffic and make a dash for the sanctuary of the grassy bank. Quickly follow it up left to the retaining wall and follow the two walls to the bottom of the crag. Bear in mind that the return dash across the carriageway is subject to reduced visibility and even more care (and sprinting speed) should be taken with this. There are now two belay bolts on the small grey slab below the routes which start in the groove above. Take a 60m rope and 15 quickdraws.

1 Iskra ★★★ F6b+

FA C. Struthers, N. Siddiqui 08.99

'*Iskra*' is Russian for spark and the title of the revolutionary newspaper but that's enough about Russian history. Follow the groove and start breaking left at the third bolt which requires a long quickdraw to avoid rope drag. Follow steepening, stepped rock to a larger overlap. Move right into a final corner and then lean left to clip new lower-offs.

2 Maximum R&B ★★ F7a

FA N. Siddiqui, C. Struthers 29.07.99

Takes the airy, steep groove direct through the overlaps to move right to a thin crack below the lower-off. Start as for Iskra but continue on the right-hand line of bolts through the guano stain to the hidden third bolt and eventually to new lower-offs.

Steve Long on Iskra, Gallery Upper Crag.
Photo Colin Struthers.

THE HISTORIES

Castle Inn

The crag was first visited by Colin Goodey and friends in the spring of 1958 and used as a training venue. At that time there was no car park, just dense vegetation and trees which made it difficult to get to the base. Top-roped ascents were made of routes 1, 2 and 3. A year later, in 1959, *Route 1* (HVS) and *Route 2* (E2) were led by Colin. There was a long wait before further development in 1982 when *Route 3*, *Cakewalk* and *Driving the Dumper* were all led at E3 by Andy Pollitt and Trevor Hodgeson. In 1984 Gary Gibson added *School Mam* at E3. In around 1991 the crag was bolted by members of *Clwyd MC* but it was not to last. Someone removed them and Colin, having taken to the bolted style and together with two members of Clwyd MC, replaced the bolts using an industrial compressor. At the same time he then filled in the last obvious line with an ascent of *Finale*. There have also been a number of minor recent additions in 2008 and 2009.

Llanddulas Cave

The first routes go back to 1984 when six trad routes were established in the **Upper Cave** area. The first four were climbed on 27/06/84: *Pearl from the Shell*, *Searching*, *P.C. Wimpout* and *Afterglow* were the work of Trevor Hodgson, S. Chesslett and P. Custy. The first routes in the **Forgotten Sun** area were climbed in 1991 and were the work of Norman Clacher and others. The first seems to have been *Field of Dreams* in April of that year. The venue was given a makeover in 1995 with a lot more sport routes appearing, especially in the **Forgotten Sun** area. The routes were largely rebolted with resin bolts by Chris Parkin in October 2007. There was a feverish burst of activity in 2008 and 2009 involving new routing, cleaning and rebolting of existing routes, many of which had their hangers removed and had not been climbed in years. The result has been an almost complete makeover and a large batch of very worthwhile routes. The activists in the latest makeover were: (in alphabetical order) Ian Andrews, Mike Burrows, Norman Clacher, Glyn Davidson, Mike Doyle, Lee Proctor and Tony Shelmerdine.

The Gallery

In 1988 **The Gallery** was first spotted by Colin Struthers and Nadim (Big Sid) Siddiqui when returning along the Marine Drive in the evening light. A quick drive around the bay revealed a lot of clean rock, a few old pegs and a bit of tat on the right-hand end of the crag but no evidence of any other climbing. The potential was duly noted and, at the end of that year, Colin and Graham Harrison of the Creag Dhu set out to climb the first route, *Intimate Strangers*. Encouraged by the quality of the climbing Colin returned in the spring with Nadim and together they began developing the crag. At the end of 1989 they produced a laminated topo with some twenty route descriptions. Despite the excellence of the climbing, the crag never became popular – many people, expecting standard bolted fare, found the dark and puzzling style of the routes intimidating. In late 2009 Colin Struthers and friends returned to undertake a major re-equipping of lower-offs and added some extra bolts. Hopefully the crag will now finally get the attention that it deserves. Penmaen-bach Point became known as Violet's Leap due to a famous and notorious incident in 1909.

The Story of Violet Charlesworth (THE GALLERY)

On 2nd January 1909, a smartly dressed woman ran eastwards into the Old Ship Inn 400 metres from Penmaen-bach Point and announced that her sister had vanished after her car had gone over the cliff. The car was found pivoting on a ledge some 50 metres from the sea and her driver was nearby pointing to the Tam-o' Shanter hat and notes which were owned by Violet Charlesworth. It was claimed that the vehicle had crashed and that Violet had been thrown from the car, over the cliffs and into the sea, but it soon emerged that all was not as it had at first appeared. In fact Violet had tried to fake her own death to extricate herself from a dire position entirely of her own making. Thereafter, the hunt was on to find her. The British nation became gripped by the affair which became known as 'The Welsh Cliff Mystery' and it was of such interest that it even appeared in the American press including the New York Times.

Details of Violet's sensational double life began to emerge. She had been claiming to be the heiress to a huge fortune and, on the strength of her brazen manner, had been granted substantial credit to pursue a lavish lifestyle. She had conned money from a number of men who fell for her enigmatic looks and she had also duped a trusting widow out of her entire life savings of £500, then a tidy sum. A few weeks before the 'tragedy', creditors had gathered at Violet Charlesworth's then current home in St Asaph in the vain hope of being paid. The occasion was to have been her 25th birthday party – but she did not make an appearance. Her furniture was seized and sold in lieu of rent owed.

Knowing that her debts were spiralling out of control, Violet had staged her death hoping to lay low for a while and re-emerge under a new identity. The ruse had worked for a time but, with the help of huge press coverage, she was eventually tracked down to Scotland and brought to trial. Violet (26) and her mother Miriam (59) were found guilty of fraud and sentenced to three years' penal servitude (prison with hard labour) in Derby gaol. Their sentences began in February 1910 and thereby transpires the biggest mystery of all. No records of their release survive, nor has any trace of the two women been found either in the press or genealogical records after they were sentenced. What did happen to Violet Charlesworth?

The Gallery activists; Dave Kells, Mark Hounslea, Colin Struthers and Kevin Stephens. (Right) Mark Hounslea on Iskra (6b+) Upper Crag.

Penmaen Head first ascentionists Francis Gowling, Norman Clacher, Ian Andrews and Tony Shelmerdine. (Right) Michael Doyle with resin gun at Flowstone Wall.

Penmaen Head

Rick Newcombe climbed here in the 1960s. In the summer of 1975, Colin Darlington and Pete White climbed what is now *Chris Corner* (severe) on **Wen Wall**. Pete led the corner and Colin led the second pitch to the top, belaying on the rotary washing line at the back of the *Hotel 70 Degrees*. The first pitch was the only clean bit of rock on the route and the ascent was also memorable as Colin managed to get his privates jammed in his harness.

DEVELOPING PENMAEN HEAD

(Michael Doyle)

Living in Holywell since 1983 and travelling along the A55 from the Orme and Snowdonia on hundreds of occasions, I had often looked up at the white limestone wall above the railway tunnel just outside of Colwyn Bay and wondered whether it was worth checking out for climbing purposes. Eventually the pull became too great and in October 2006 I parked in the lay-by beside the then derelict Hotel 70 Degrees and walked down the steps on the public footpath. An extensive crag complex slowly revealed itself, most of it hidden from view from the expressway by the trees.

Expressway Wall aside, the whole complex was heavily vegetated and overgrown with ivy. Below **Penmaenrhos Wall** there was a lot of brush and branches had to be snapped off just to walk under the crag. **Expressway Wall** itself was extremely clean and composed of the most amazing, rough limestone. I could hardly believe what I had found considering how obvious it was from the road. The potential was in no doubt and it was very exciting. Being wary of spending a lot of money and time in developing the venue only to experience access problems, I contacted the BMC access officer who checked the place out on a visit to North Wales and subsequently advised that approaching the owners (if

📷 Mike Doyle drilling what was to become The Double Helix (F6a+) on Flowstone Wall. Photo Chris Doyle. (Right) Francis Gowling on Expressway Wall. Photo Michael Doyle.

they could be found) to get permission would likely cause more problems that it would solve. The plunge was taken and a load of Fixe Inox bolts from Planet Fear were duly ordered and a heavy duty battery drill and resin were bought.

▌▌ With my son Chris, we started developing **Penmaenrhos Wall**, removing the ivy and installing a rope for access to the ledges above. On a subsequent visit we were puzzled to find that this rope had disappeared as we did not believe either climbers (part of a tatty old climbing rope) or kids (too dangerous to retrieve) would be interested. We were proved wrong when sometime after a bunch of kids turned up from the nearby Tan y Lan estate with the rope around the shoulders of one and proceeded to solo up the ledges to the top of the crag while using it to haul up bottles of lemonade!

▌▌ Though keen to maintain a low profile, we were drawn by the easier pickings on **Flowstone Wall** to the left and this sector was the first to be fully developed. After cleaning, removal of loose rock and checking the moves, the first bolts were installed on three routes on 09/03/07 at the left of the crag and these routes had their first ascent the day after. These were *Richard II 1399* (F6a), *Big up the Lizard* (F5+) and *Tan y Lan Kids* (F5) – the first sport route at **Penmaen Head**. The quality of the climbing was encouraging and another seven routes quickly followed, which were all found to be worthwhile and in the F6 category. We shared first ascents with Chris doing the harder routes such as the classic *Flowstone Shuffle* 6b+ and *Fixe Inox City* (6b+).

▌▌ On completion of **Flowstone Wall**, in August of 2007, **Wen Wall** first received attention and required quite a lot of work. Loose rock was removed as was the soil and vegetation on the finishing ledge. This wall turned out to give five short but excellent routes between severe and F6c. Mike Burrows and myself shared first ascents in October and November of 2007. At around this time I started work on **Expressway Wall**, leaving this to the end as it is so visible from the A55 expressway and the game would truly be up within a very short period.

" Norman Clacher discovered the development on a chance visit on New Year's Day 2008. He rang up local guru Tony Shelmerdine who knew nothing about it but the issue was discussed with Norman one night at Prestatyn climbing wall and he was shown around early in January of that year. He was keen to assist with development and in regular visits over only four months, assisted by Ian Andrews, had established fifteen routes, mainly on **Penmaenrhos Wall** with the first routes coming on the right-hand end in February 2008. This represented a lot of work, removing much loose rock and ivy. Norman and Tony Shelmerdine also established two of the harder and longest routes (*70 Degrees*, F6c and *Clogau Gold*, F7a) on the right of **Railway Tunnel Wall**

and in February and March of 2008 he also worked out *Red Wall* with assistance from Ian Andrews and Tony Shelmerdine. Ria Roberts established the excellent *Snowdrop* (6a+) on **Railway Tunnel Wall** in February 2008.

" **Expressway Wall** was developed from February to May 2008. The wall provided eleven routes, all of which turned out to be worthwhile and some very much so. First ascents were shared between me, Ian Andrews, Chris Doyle, and Mike Burrows. On 09.04.08, Ian Andrews and I bagged *Ryan's Route* (F6a+) which takes a nice line up the vague central groove. Other highlights included *Paranoia Crack* (F6b), (22.04.08), the obvious crack/groove on the right of the crag named after the paranoia that creeps in while new routing that someone else may steal your routes. Also on 24.04.08, the excellent *The Mankind Initiative* (F6b) with some good but steep finishing moves was established. Mike Burrows bagged *Adam's Exams* – the fine crack to the right of *Paranoia Crack* at F6a+. Managing to temporarily drag Chris away kicking and screaming from his bizarre bouldering fixation, he climbed the technical *That's Enough New Routes for Now* but going right

GENERAL HISTORY

After returning from a campaign in Ireland, King Richard II was kidnapped by the forces of Henry Bolingbroke on **Penmaen Head** in 1399. He surrendered in Conway Castle after talks with the Earl of Northumberland. The king passed into Bolingbroke's custody in the Tower. Bolingbroke demanded that he relinquish the throne and pass it to Bolingbroke by right of succession in the male line, following noble and European tradition. The king abdicated under pressure on 29 September 1399, bringing his twenty-two year reign to an end. He was taken to Pontefract Castle. The failure of another loyalist

plot reminded Henry of Lancaster how great a liability the live Richard would be. By the end of February 1400, Richard of Bordeaux had been starved to death. Henry Bolingbroke proclaimed himself king and took the throne as Henry IV. It is not recorded whether Richard had the opportunity to do any crag development work while in the area.

Penmaen Head was once a true sea cliff and the rock between the sea and back to the edge of **Expressway Wall** (the area through which the A55 expressway now passes) has been quarried away over the years. That's

at the second bolt at F7a. Immediately to the right he bagged *Fathers for Justice* (F6c). Chris also climbed *Kneeshaw Lupton* (the route to the left of *The Mankind Initiative*) at around F6c+ but with a thin and somewhat sustained second half, finishing up the groove.

" The line finishing at the prow to the left of *Ryan's Route* looked improbable at a reasonable grade and consequently was left to last. After taking a whipper due to pulling a small flake off, it went at a surprisingly reasonable F6b+ on 30.06.08. *The Quarrywoman*, as it became, turned out to be top notch, so much so that it required its own lower-off.

" While Norman Clacher and Ian Andrews continued with the development of **Penmaenrhos Wall**, northern raiders Colin Struthers and friends turned up and somewhat controversially established three routes on that wall in mid July of 2008. On 26.07.08 Tony Shelmerdine had the last and hardest route to date at **Penmaen Head** with the very steep *Sir Crimpalot* at 7a+. To all intents and purposes the complex is now fully developed and in a mere seventeen months from first to last route.

" The arrangement was that whoever did the first ascent, paid for equipping the route. I had an outstanding first ascent to do on **Railway Tunnel Wall** (which became *Pier Pressure – £10 down*) when a head emerged over the top – step forward one Francis Gowling. "That'll cost you a tenner" the head was gravely informed. He was less than pleased regarding it as being £10 down on the climb and replied that he didn't have any money on him due to being "Like the Queen".

" It has meant a lot of work as the venue was highly vegetated with ivy and brambles and had its share of loose rock but the routes are now solid. Much loose rock was also removed from above the climbs to improve safety. Better down than up. Francis Gowling liked it so much he clocked up twenty-seven consecutive days, having to tear himself away to go on a climbing trip to Kalymnos! Nine members of the Clwyd Mountaineering Club subsequently assisted with a clean-up of the approaches, collecting 10 bags of garbage. It has been very satisfying. Having now caught the crag development bug in a big way there are another couple of pristine crags in the pipeline – watch this space. "

a lot of rock! Before the Hotel 70 Degrees was built on top of **Penmaen Head** in 1972, there were three quarrymen's stone cottages on the site which included the foreman's house and that of the quarry manager. The cottages were pulled down in the mid-1950s when the Penmaenrhos quarry owners, Kneeshaw Lupton, decided to extend the quarry to the other side of the 482 metres long railway tunnel. It was eventually decided this would be too dangerous because the tunnel might collapse (and so **Expressway Wall** was spared). Kneeshaw Lupton had their own railway siding nearby and the remains of its loading jetty can still be seen on the pebble beach below. The quarry closed in 1960 and new houses and the Hotel 70 Degrees were built. The hotel was built on a metal frame into the rock and was called the Hotel 70 Degrees because everything was constructed at a 70 degree angle – the walls, the floors, and the stairs. If you walk down below the Hotel site, you'll find a vent from the railway tunnel for the old steam trains.

Chris Doyle making the first ascent of
Flowstone Shuffle (F6b+ ***) on Flowstone
Wall at Penmaen Head on 20/08/07.
Photo Michael Doyle.

Route Index